# TALES OF ICELAND

-OR-

## "RUNNING WITH THE HULDUFÓLK IN THE PERMANENT DAYLIGHT"

**STEPHEN MARKLEY**

GIVELIVEEXPLORE
PUBLISHING

GIVELIVEEXPLORE, LLC
Tales of Iceland or "Running with the Huldufólk in the Permanent Daylight"
Stephen Markley

Copyright © 2013 by Stephen Markley
All Rights Reserved

Illustrations © 2013 by SiggaRún
All Rights Reserved
For more of SiggaRún's work, visit siggarune.com

Cover Design: Benjamin Osborn
Interior Illustrator: SiggaRún
Interior Design: Matthew Trinetti

All rights reserved. This book was published by GiveLiveExplore, LLC. No
part of this book may be reproduced in any form by any means without the
express permission of the publisher and author. This includes reprints, excerpts,
photocopying, recording, or any future means of reproducing text.

Please seek permission first and contact us at TalesofIceland.com/contact if you
would like to do any of the above.

Published in the United States by GiveLiveExplore, LLC
978-0-9892165-1-7

Version 1.0

If you're an author, writer, or traveler and would like to work with
GiveLiveExplore, email Matt@GiveLiveExplore.com.

**5% of all profits from this book are donated to SEEDS Iceland.**

SEEDS is an Icelandic non-governmental, non-profit volunteer organization designed to promote intercultural understanding, environmental protection and awareness through work on environmental, social and cultural projects within Iceland. Each year, SEEDS hosts hundreds of volunteers from all over the world to work on environmental projects around Iceland. SEEDS also sends Icelandic volunteers to work on humanitarian and environmental projects abroad.

For the people of Iceland,
we enjoyed singing "Thong Song" with you.

# Contents

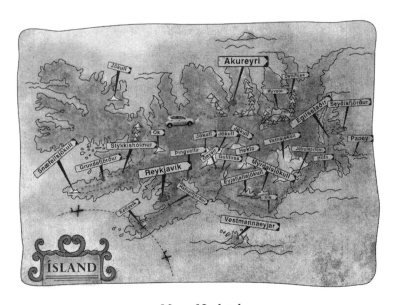

**Map of Iceland**
Illustration © SiggaRún, 2013

# ONE

# Why Iceland

Why anywhere? It's unclear how the places we wish to travel get stuck in our heads as destinations on a kind of epic, global to-do list—most of which will never get done before worms are sucking out our eyeballs. I know that stored in my imagination I have a panoply of countries, cities, vistas, monuments, spider holes, canteens, hallowed grounds, and myriad other *Planet Earth* destinations I'm always telling myself I'll get to eventually. God help us if interstellar travel ever works out and suddenly we add multiple planets and solar systems to that to-do list in our to-be memory.

With Iceland, however, I remember the exact moment I decided I had to get there. I was in college and Quentin Tarantino was on *Late Night with Conan O'Brien* raving about his New Year's Eve experience in Iceland. "Supermodels working at McDonald's," was the phrase that understandably stuck with me. Previously, I knew basically nothing about the country except that its capital city was Reykjavík and it wasn't as cold as Greenland.

**[This is the one piece of knowledge-that-shouldn't-count-as-knowledge everyone retains about Iceland: that the Vikings switched the**

names of Greenland and Iceland in hopes of tricking everybody as to which place to call home. Historically, this is probably kinda-sorta accurate in the superficial, elementary school-level way—as roughly accurate as, "The founding fathers were all great men."]

Tarantino—spastic, emphatic, and on *Conan* to promote the release of a film he'd produced that served the sole purpose of allowing viewers to watch young people get sadistically tortured to death—planted a bug in my brain that never wormed its way out. I was a college kid who enjoyed getting drunk and attempting to sleep with beautiful women, so how could his endorsement not stick?

[**Sooo much has changed since those days. For instance: Now I have this weird patch of hair that grows out of an otherwise hairless quadrant of my abdomen and I'm terrified to shave or pluck it for fear it will expand or coarsen. It's a totally different world.**]

That movie he was promoting was called *Hostel*. I remember sitting in the theater watching this film where outlandishly beautiful women lured young kids into torture chambers to get their thumbs cut off and their thighs drilled full of holes and their eyeballs pulled out of their sockets. As they screamed, I kept thinking to myself in icy-cool-blue lettering with mist rising around the edges: *Icccccee-Laaaaaand*.

After that, a whole bunch of shit happened.

I graduated from college, I traveled the country, I moved to Chicago, I got a job, I published my first book, I quit the job, I traveled some more, I wrote more books, I saw *Hostel II*. Through it all, I never really considered traveling to Iceland; it just sat in the back of my mind, unrealized. It's strange the way that opportunity arises in life, the way forces can coincide and align. Here is the unremarkable story of how I ended up actually going to Iceland, but first you have to know about a couple of friends of mine, who will both go by bastardized versions of their last names.

**[Although I'm about to do a really terrible job of protecting their identities, and by the end of this you should easily be able to Facebook both and follow them on Twitter.]**

## "You're not leaving us in suspense are you, you sonofabitch?"

—Trin, to Bojo when Bojo said aloud that he wasn't sure if he would take a shower in the morning.

To understand my friend Trin, it's really best if you've seen the two NBC sitcoms *30 Rock* and *Parks and Recreation*. Trin is kind of a hybrid of Rob Lowe's Chris Traeger, and Jon Hamm as Liz Lemon's two-episode boyfriend: this incredibly handsome dude with black hair, bright blue-gray eyes, a concoction of dark Greek and Italian features, strong build, resplendent smile.

**[Of course I'm comfortable enough in my sexuality to call another guy's smile "resplendent." I also have a Sarah McLachlan song on my iTunes—"World on Fire"—so eat me.]**

Like Jon Hamm on *30 Rock*, he's this handsome guy who just does not understand that his handsomeness gives him great advantages in life. From women to work to socializing, the indefatigable aura of swoon produced by the red-giant star of his handsome carries him across the universe with rainbows trailing. He never seems to understand that it's not normal for a guy to walk into a bar and have every attractive woman stumble over themselves to talk to him. He just can't comprehend that for the rest of normal-looking-guy humanity, smiling resplendently won't cause panties to dissolve in moisture across a 50-mile radius.

Yet the great (or terrible, depending on your perspective) thing about Trin is that his good looks do not manifest in his personality as arrogance and entitlement and cruelty the way they can in certain people. Like Chris Traeger, his optimism and love of life are the two most prominent qualities to his personality. He's just a really, really nice guy. A really nice guy, who played center for his high school football team, studied engineering at Georgia Tech and worked as a consultant for IBM. To be sure, all this could be totally obnoxious. Everyone knows a person who's just too annoyingly kind and great and perfect to the point where you think it's either bullshit and he's a child molester or, even worse, not bullshit. Luckily (or unluckily), Trin has just enough of an edge to round him out. He's funny but in that really weird way that makes a person refreshingly normal. For instance, his farts smell like the aftermath of a nuclear holocaust, and he giggles every time he births one.

In 2011, Trin decided he needed to try something new; he'd been at his job at IBM for five years, and he got to the point where, "I was either going to keep going along, heading down that path or I was going to try to do something I always wanted to do." He went to his supervisors and told them he wanted to quit, and they gave him a seven-month leave of absence instead—as if that had nothing to do with dropping that resplendent smile, the stupid, beautiful fuck.

# "We should have told them we're not typical cruise-ship D-bags. We're on-land D-bags."

—Bojo, on how we better could have seduced two cruise ship dancers we met in a coffee shop, who, we figured, were probably only impressed by good-looking D-bags on their cruise ship.

I don't think I exchanged more than five words with Bojo during the first six months I knew him. The guy is preternaturally quiet even when surrounded by his best friends. At parties, he can blend into the conversation and stand without saying a word for so long that you wonder if he's had a stroke. For someone who enjoys talking out of his ass so much that it's kind of a waste my mouth is located on my face, this is beyond my ken. Our mutual friends and I often wonder what he's thinking about in these moments, if he's actually deep in thought about the ether-bound mysteries of the universe or if he's just humming in his head to the *Rawhide* theme, "Bojo-Bojo-Bojo! Bojo-Bojo-Bojo! Bojoooo!"

But then you get to know the kid and slowly discover that not only is he an incredibly intelligent guy, but he also has that weird sense of humor, with an innate ability to say something so perfectly goofy and irreverent at the exact right moment. I always tell him that he likes to save it up, to say nothing for two hours of a five-hour car ride and then hit you with the off-the-cuff remark at the precise moment you're least able to resist it. Taking it back to NBC sitcoms, he's Costanza making the one crack at the boardroom meeting, throwing up his hands, and leaving the room. He also recently grew a full, dark, jealousy-inducing beard, which one of my female friends in Chicago observed made him my second hottest friend (guess who took first?).

Bojo, also an engineer, worked in the suburbs of Chicago for a manufacturer, designing parts for big industrial firms like Caterpillar, which is about as outside of my understanding as IBM consulting or not speaking for an hour. His commute from the city took an hour there and an hour and a half back. This kind of daily slog meant he woke at 6 a.m. and rarely got home before 7 p.m. One can only keep up that kind of schedule for so long before either going crazy or marrying someone awful and moving to the suburb where he works. So Bojo applied to grad school and decided on the MBA program at Carnegie Mellon in Pittsburgh. This meant he too would be quitting his job, and it just seemed clever to quit before the summer began to join Trin for a few months on his trip. After an exhaustive search (you will quickly learn that these two are into researching things "exhaustively" before plunging in, which only begins to define the wonderful differences in our personalities), they found a cheap flight to Reykjavík on Icelandair.

## Enter Markley

Unlike Bojo and Trin, I wasn't quitting a job or going back to school. I'd been underemployed for a year or more, was in the middle of working on my second and third books simultaneously and had just lucked into the fattest fiscal windfall of my life when I sold the movie rights to *Publish This Book*. Without going into the biography of this period too much, I'll say that I basically used the cash to 1) stop scrapping for freelance gigs to focus on book writing for as long as I could and 2) take as many pretty girls out on dates as I could possibly fit into waking hours.

**[This had its benefits and drawbacks. For instance, it got expensive to have four dates in a week, plus two weekend nights on the town that lasted till 4 a.m. in order to find fodder for more dates. It only dawned on me that I was going to blow through this relatively meager movie money way too fast when I bought an extremely pretty 41-year-old divorcée (who clearly was an adult person who made more money than me) $100 worth of casual drinks on a Tuesday night.]**

I also wanted to use the money to take a trip somewhere I'd never been before, and when Bojo and Trin mentioned that they'd bought tickets to Iceland, I flashed back to that long-ago endorsement from the producer of *Hostel*. Within a few weeks I'd found a $600 ticket on Icelandair.

## What This Book Is Not

Before we get to our story, we have to go over a few things this book is not so that no one is upset when they begin to understand that I have no recommendations for Reykjavík fine dining, nor do I understand how to say, "Which way is the potato farm?" or any other Icelandic phrase. I know nothing about Iceland other than what I've gleaned from my travels and read on the Internet or in this archeologically fascinating educatio-informatensil of our near past called a "bok."

**[My editor says the correct spelling is "book" but we will have to agree to disagree.]**

This is not a guide. I know no other routes in Iceland other than the one I took, and I know no other destinations and sights other than the ones I saw.

If I had to classify this, I'd call it travel lit with a distinctly Markleyian flare—"Markleyian" being the definition of any weird little fucking thing that comes into my head stirred with narrative and sociopolitical whining.

There will be stories that have nothing to do with Iceland. There will be vastly inappropriate jokes about body functions and functions the body was never intended to undertake, and many of these will not be all that funny if you weren't there.

This is also not a "backpacker's guide" to shit. I did not live in Iceland for six months. I didn't even have a backpacker's backpack. I had a little rolly-type suitcase my mom gave me several years ago, which I wheeled around loudly over cobblestones looking very mom-like. My actual backpack I'd just gotten for free from a friend, and it drew me only because of its sheer number of pockets. For some reason I find multiple pockets a very attractive feature of a backpack, especially because my actual backpacker's backpack, which I've lugged around on so many previous trips, is this Osprey with just one massive pocket for everything, so all your clothes, books, toiletries, and other possessions just end up in a savage muddle. Though they sell a lot of merchandise, I would gladly enter an Oxford-style debate to argue that Osprey doesn't know dick about backpacks.

I took a 2½-week trip and, let's face it: if you're a debt-loaded postgrad in this uncertain economy you probably have to parcel out your travels uneasily and even 2½ weeks seems like a luxury of gargantuan proportions.

So if you've bought this book, just know that it will be a little foul. It will not teach you anything about Iceland that you can't look up on Wikipedia. It may make you laugh, but people who claim in the first chapter that the reader will laugh are usually assholes. My hope is not only that somehow, someway this becomes the indispensable book that cool people read before or during a trip to Iceland, but that perhaps it inspires more people to travel to Iceland. All I can say with full credibility is that I went to Iceland and kind of fell in love with the place. This is how it happened.

# Two

# The First 72 Hours

*I begin my journey to Iceland today, and I leave you all with this one quote that pretty much sums up everything: "I would have made a good pope." -Richard Nixon, 37th president*

—Stephen Markley, Facebook wall comment

I sat on the idling FlyBus at the Keflavík airport, Iceland's only international airport, waiting for it to take me into Reykjavík, which is about 45 minutes away. The gravelly rumbling of the bus vibrated my eyes in their sockets. It was midnight Iceland time and God-knows-what my time. I'd slept about four hours the night before, yet when the bus finally began its cruise northeast up the highway, I couldn't have felt more wide awake. I tried to read, but quickly put my book away and sat in silence with the other late-arriving passengers just watching this new land through the window.

The light situation was a dim, dusk-ish, deep blue hue on this first week of June, and I noted the small outcroppings of buildings and apartments as we drove. Passing by the lava fields covered with their sickly green lichen, watching the horizon flow and ebb as Reykjavík's suburbs grew nearer, I felt that indelible excitement rising in my chest—the kind you always get when you land in a foreign place and the possibilities of adventure are yet mere dreams in your imagination. Maybe my imagination had gone especially haywire though, because I'd already lost any delineation of the last three days. I'd spent the last nine hours traveling, whether by plane or subway or AirTran, blinking away my sleeplessness, iPod headphones getting tangled in baggage straps, terrible overpriced airport grilled-vegetable sandwiches, uncomfortable bowel movements that you intuit as the incorrect size given your recent food and alcohol intake, stale Starbucks coffee, ever-hassled at airport security.

[The less said about airport security the better, though this seems like the perfect place for a rant: What no one seemed to learn after the successful attacks of 9/11 was that they were pulled off with tools you'd barely get in trouble bringing to elementary school, and every time airport security reacts to a perceived threat—such as introducing body scans after the so-called "underwear bomber"—any not-a-fucking-idiot terrorist will presumably also react by attempting a tactic airport security has not thought of, such as sewing a bomb into their stomachs or simply gaining access to one of the millions of private jets where no one is screened at all. It's the whole "closing the barn door after the horse is out" conundrum. Meanwhile, there is now a catalog of X-ray dick pics out there to rival anything quarterback Brett Favre ever managed. Don't think for a second all those nude photos aren't ending up in some guy's whack-off folder.]

If you're ever flying to Europe, however, it is imperative that you check Icelandair first before subjecting yourself to the intractable hellscape of a Delta or United (more on this momentarily).

Not only was I flying to Iceland for the bargain basement price of $600 round-trip, but Icelandair is its own kind of Euro-Nordic paradise with remarkable legroom, pretty flight attendants with cool flight-attendant hats, and touch-screen, multi-choice entertainment systems. One of the things that consistently annoys us all about the in-flight movie situation is that you're sometimes stuck with one crappy choice or several crappy choices usually in the vein of a Katherine Heigl rom-com or disposable Jason Statham action flick in which he kicks an improbable number of people without ever being shot. On Icelandair there were not only more than 40 choices of film (not to mention music, including a Sigur Rós station, TV shows, and Iceland documentaries), but you can pause the goddamn thing in the middle. You know how many key plot points of that Johnny Depp-as-Dillinger movie I missed because I had to take a piss?

[After gushing about this in-flight movie situation to anyone who would listen, many, many people informed me that this is more or less the norm for international flights now, but whatever, man—I remain impressed. I chose to catch up on my 2011 Oscar noms with the George Clooney vehicle *The Descendants*. It is inarguably true that even though George Clooney only ever plays George Clooney, he is indelibly great in that role, and *The Descendents* in particular evoked a kind of winsome, mystic Clooneyness that I found greatly affecting. For my second choice, I moved on to the unintentionally hilarious Oliver Stone shithouse sequel *Wall Street: Money Never Sleeps*. If you missed it in theaters, I highly recommend it. It's the quintessential unnecessary sequel, with the iconic character of Gordon Gekko reduced to a vacillation between a Danny Ocean con artist and touchy-feely grandpa, but the bulk of the film is carried by Shia LeBeouf as the

Charlie Sheen-naïf biting off more than he can chew Wall-Street-wise (Shia LeBeouf, it should be noted, doesn't have the gravitas to carry a Bounty paper towel commercial). The only downside to this is that I started the second film too late, and the plane landed in Keflavík Airport with 10 minutes left, so I never did find out if money, in fact, ever slept.]

Yet we have to back up. Because in order to understand just how fried my brain was after the first 72 hours I spent in Iceland, I have to begin with this story even though it has literally zero relevance to anything Iceland related. This story is the nexus—the jumping-off point—for experiencing the kind of sleep deprivation usually associated with the first Afghans we caught after 9/11 who had to stand on boxes for days straight while CIA dogs barked at them.

My Icelandair flight was out of JFK, the least accessible airport in the contiguous U.S., which, stupidly, just meant that eventually I had to find my way to New York City.

[When buying flights overseas, I tend to envision everything east of the Mississippi as "where I live" and therefore easy and cheap enough to reach one way or the other without worrying about it until the week before the trip.]

New York City, however, is also home to one of my oldest friends, Ian, with whom I find it constitutionally impossible to not get fucked up out of my mind when we are together. We are extremely bad influences on each other.

What happened was this: I had a flight from O'Hare to White Plains airport in Westchester, N.Y., which was the most accessible airport for Ian to pick me up. My United flight left O'Hare around

4 p.m. and was supposed to get into White Plains at 7 p.m. This flight was one of those bad dreams with the cliché of the screaming 3-year-old whose lungs didn't tire the entire two hours until—get this—20 minutes away from landing the pilots discovered that the "flaps were not deploying." Now maybe you're a Boeing engineer and immediately understand what this means, but all the people on this United flight did not and the way the flight attendant doled out the information could not have been scripted to accrete more tension.

"What this means," the flight attendant said, "is that we can't slow down before we land."

[Passengers' eyes widen, sharp inhales.]

"We can still land, but White Plains doesn't have a long enough runway."

[So we're all fucked? passengers wonder. We're going to die because White Plains skimped on its fucking runway length?]

"The closest runway that's long enough for this kind of landing is O'Hare."

[Oh, so we'll live, but this is going to be really annoying.]

"And don't worry we have enough fuel."

[Yeah, that didn't even occur to me, but now I'm retroactively worried past my relief.]

"The landing is going to be a little different than you're used to; we'll be coming in pretty fast and hard."

[We are going to die, aren't we, you fucking liar? Also, that's what she said.]

"There will be fire trucks and ambulances there to greet us when we land, but they're just a precaution."

**[Jesus Christ.]**

As you can imagine, by the time we landed in Chicago surrounded by fire trucks and ambulances, deplaned, replaned on a new plane, and flew back to White Plains, a certain *Lost* syndrome had taken over, in which you cannot help but bond with your immediate passenger-mates who are also suffering through this shitty airline experience to the point where you're all ready to go in search of the Smoke Monster. Ian picked me up at midnight, greeting me with a half-hour rant that went approximately like: "Fucking Markley, who the fuck do you think you are? Mr. Hollywood—Mr. Fucking Hollywood! Sells one movie script and thinks he can fly in on his private jet whenever he feels like it and the whole world will just act as his chauffeur, like I don't have anything better to do but wait at the airport for five hours while you get your ass licked on George Clooney's yacht, you piece of shit. Fuck you. Let's get drunk."

The night proceeded as if it was going to be a bust. Ian and I drank tall boys out of brown paper bags on the A train and hurtled down to the West Village where we played pool, slammed $3 Pabst, and generally tried to make something of our failing night. We decided to wander over to a favorite bar of mine called White Horse Tavern only to discover it was closed. This was at about 3:30 a.m., and I saw that a small bar across the street called WBEX Radio was still open so we ducked in there only to discover that there appeared to be no good-looking girls at all. There were two guys at the bar and a couple of small groups in the booths by the window—maybe 11 total still drinking at that hour. We sat at the bar, ordered beers, and I bought Ian tequila to make up for my late flight. Only then did I notice that none other than Kiefer Sutherland—the Kiefer Sutherland of *Flatliners*, *Lost Boys*, and most notably, Jack Bauer fame—was sitting in the corner booth with some friends. It wasn't even one of those things where you have to squint and wonder if you're seeing someone famous because he was that close and that distinctly Kiefer Sutherland-looking.

"Holy shit," I said to Ian. "That's not even close to not being Kiefer Sutherland."

"Yep," said Ian, nodding in appreciation. "That's for sure Kiefer Sutherland."

We had a pleasant, too-sober discussion about how we were just not the kind of people who would ever approach a famous person to say hi because there's something distinctly tacky and needy in doing that. Maybe if it was someone I fucking worshipped like your basic Springsteen or your Civil Rights legend Congressman John Lewis, my awe would kick into overdrive and I wouldn't be able to help it, but we were not about to do anything except tell our friends and family that we once saw Kiefer Sutherland drinking in a bar at 3:30 a.m. I loved *24*, even after it became a parody of itself, so I was pretty stoked for this. Certainly I could at least turn it into a short blog post. He appeared to be with a small group of friends, maybe two guys and a woman, although this all became consumed in the fog of what happened next.

The bartender called last call, and Kiefer got up to order one last shot. Ian and I were finishing our beers, and as he approached the short end of the L-shaped bar, we were obviously going to watch him take this shot. There were two guys beside us—pretty evidently boyfriends on a date— maybe just having a nightcap before they went home, and the smaller, slenderer of the two—a kid who maybe came up to my collarbone if he stood on his tiptoes—suddenly got all bold and said, across us, to Kiefer, "You should buy shots for the whole bar."

He said this as Kiefer was in the midst of taking this shot (maybe Jaeger, but uncertain), and he slugged it back the way he would in a movie and slapped the glass back down with two fingers. His eyes rose lazily upward and came to rest on the kid. There was this really long beat during which he just stared at the kid and everyone in the bar stared at him.

Then Kiefer Sutherland goes, "What the fuck did you just say to me?"

I laughed because I thought he was joking. Then I shut my mouth.

"You want me to fucking buy shots for the bar, you stupid fuck?" he said, voice rising. "Who the fuck do you think you are? Maybe you want to go outside. Maybe you want to go outside and see what the fuck is up, huh?"

He had this really vicious, grinding edge to his voice, the kind he had when he was torturing Arabs to find out the location of nuclear footballs and such. His friend, the woman, patted him on the shoulder and said, "C'mon, let's go."

"No, fuck this guy!" screamed Kiefer. "Fucking big man hot shit fucking piece of shit. *Fuck you, asshole! You fucking loser. Fuck you!*"

And Kiefer Sutherland was, like, *screaming* at this kid, who just sat there taking it. Maybe he tried to stammer an apology at first, but Kiefer's rage was just so white hot, so disproportionate to the relatively innocuous comment the kid just off-handedly let loose, probably because he was simply attempting to think of an excuse to engage a celebrity in conversation without seeming like a drooling plebe asking for an autograph.

"You fucking pissant! You fucking piece of shit, you want me to buy you a fucking shot? Let's step outside, man; let's see who's buying a fucking shot!" he roared, and then he bounded out of the bar, throwing the door wide so that it crashed against the building, and he was gone. Everybody in the bar was wide eyed and looking at each other like, *What the hell just happened? Did Kiefer Sutherland just freak out in front of—*

And then Kiefer Sutherland comes crashing back into the bar, striding straight toward this kid, shouting, *"NO FUCKING WAY, MAN! YOU FUCKING FUCK TELL ME TO BUY A FUCKING SHOT!"*

Now you have to understand, the bar stool situation looked like this, from left to right:

**[Boyfriend] - [Guy Kiefer Sutherland Is Going To Beat the Fuck Out Of] - [Me] - [Ian]**

So Kiefer kind of shoved in right between me and this guy who'd suggested Kiefer buy shots for the bar, and he was in full-blown Jack Bauer, "tell-me-where-the-detonator-is!" mode.

*"LET'S GO OUTSIDE, ASSHOLE I WILL FUCK YOU UP! I WILL FUCKING FUCK UP YOUR LIFE!"*

And his friends were back in there because Kiefer was raging, raging drunk and smelled like a shipment of rye whiskey crashed into a moonshine distillery; they were gently tapping him on the shoulder, telling him, "C'mon, man, it's not worth it. C'mon, let's just go home," and it was comical because Kiefer Sutherland is not a tall man, maybe 5 feet 8 inches, and he was screaming at this tiny gay kid.

**[Who, let me make clear, I think Kiefer had no idea was gay. In fact, in Kiefer's drunken state it appeared he was taking this kid wearing a '50s-style V-neck for some kind of *West Side Story* tough. At least, that was as plausible as anything happening at the moment.]**

And it was pretty hard to not find this all incredibly bewildering and amusing. I thought I was stifling a smile, but Ian later told me that I was just flat-out cracking up at the bar, covering my mouth and kind of watching Kiefer carry on without offering any help whatsoever. But not laughing suddenly got way harder because then this star of film and television stuffed a cigarette in his mouth, stepped back, and started flailing his arms around in waves, and—I fucking kid you not—slipped into an Irish accent.

"Aye, ya thank you're so facking special, do ya? You stupid fack! You stupid facking piece-a shite, I'll facking take you outside and fack up your world, boy-o!"

And I was thinking to myself: *Is Kiefer Sutherland speaking in an Irish accent? Is this really happening? Does he have any kind of Irish ancestry or is he making fun of this kid because he thinks the kid's Irish?*

"Yoy! Ya facking smiling, shite-eating fack!" he went on, arms undulating in waves. "I'll see ya outside, boy-o!"

And then his friends finally convinced Kiefer to follow them, and he went back to his normal American accent, shouting, "Fuck you!" multiple times the rest of the way out of the bar.

When he was gone, Ian and I just kind of exchanged this look like, *That was the coolest thing I've ever seen, and thank God for the broken flaps on my plane.*

The two boyfriends hung back, and Ian and I slipped out of the bar to find Kiefer outside with his friends smoking a cigarette.

I didn't really know what to say, but the situation seemed to warrant something. So I go (and I promise you I'm not making this up), "Hey, man, loved you in *Melancholia*. That movie was great."

And Kiefer Sutherland kind of looked at me with this huge jack-o'-lantern grin that wrapped around his cigarette, and then he jerked his head once in a cocky, aggressive nod and said, "Fuck yeah. You're fucking-a right it was!"

And that's the kind of book about Iceland this book about Iceland is.

## Okay, But Right, This Book Is About Iceland

Pulling in to the main bus station, I was struck by the absence of skyscrapers. The entire city of Reykjavík has the height and majesty of an Akron suburb. It's so small that after de-bussing, FlyBus just popped about seven of us onto a smaller bus and drove everyone straight to their hotel or hostel, and some of these places were so close to the bus station that it felt like we'd just driven a couple of honeymooners to the end of the driveway. Finally, at around 1 a.m., I arrived at the KEX Hostel.

Bojo and Trin had arrived two days earlier, and I was in the process of figuring out the fistful of Icelandic krónur handed back to me after I checked in (I took 10,000 krónur out of the ATM, which could have either emptied my bank account or been the equivalent of an Icelandic $2 bill for all I knew) when they materialized on the back porch, all dark facial hair and American-ness spilling out of their grins.

"Whoa!" we all said, hugging, slapping backs.

"Sorry it took me so long to get in, I was unaware that you had to land and take a bus ride and then stop at everyone's hotel."

"Yeah, we kind of figured," said Bojo. "The same thing happened to us."

"Are you drunk?"

"Sort of," said Bojo. "We found a Monday-night drinking club, but all the bars close at 1 on weekdays."

"We were talking to some moderately attractive Canadian girls," said Trin.

"Moderately," Boj agreed. "We couldn't tell if they were boring."

"You're bored by everything," Trin told Bojo. "We've just been going from situation to situation that Mike finds boring. We should have taken a $600 flight to Ohio."

**["Mike" is Bojo's first name. I'm doing a seriously bad job at concealing identities.]**

I was starving, but the only thing open in Reykjavík at that hour was a 7-11-style store called "10-11" where I bought a protein bar and a ham-and-egg sandwich. I ate as we sat on the back porch of the hostel and the sky brightened.

"Is this as dark as it gets?" I asked.

"Yeah, and you can tell it's getting lighter out," said Bojo. "It's not even the height of summer yet so the nights will just keep getting shorter and shorter."

"So, what do the people do here in the winter? Just blow their fucking brains out?"

"A guy we talked to was telling us that in the winter everyone just goes to bars and plays music," said Trin.

"So, in the winter it's too dark to do anything but drink, and in the summer it's too bright out to go to sleep . . . "

"So they all drink, yes," said Trin. "And all the girls are blond. It's like Steve Markley's dream world."

**[I'll note here that most of my friends think I have an unreasonable attraction to skinny blonde girls, which, like many stereotypes (such as "all Canadians are boring" or "all Taiwanese people love pizza cookies"), has some grounding in truth.]**

"What's our game plan? I know we're here tomorrow night."

"Right," said Bojo. "Then we have the rental car reserved for Wednesday through the following Friday."

"And we just drive around the fucking island," I said.

"And we just drive around the fucking island," said Trin. "We go see some Icelandic motherfuckers doing Icelandic things. Talk to some elves. See some geysers. Real Icelandic shit."

"Who's driving? I want to drive," I said.

"Well, do you know how to drive stick?" asked Bojo. "I can, but Trin can't."

"Yeah, see when I was 17 I decided I didn't want to be a helpless pussy-ass baby squalling on the ground like a little worthless shit-for-brains," I explained. "So I just went ahead and learned how to drive a manual transmission, but so, Trin, I guess you're OK with being 25 percent less of a man? Is that correct?"

"It brings me down to an even 100 percent."

"It's really only fair," said Bojo.

Not long after that, the two of them left to try to get some sleep. I begged them to stay up with me, but it was nothing doing. I sat up in KEX's main room reading a book and watching an NBA playoff game via GameCast update on my iPad. Finally, I went to my 10-person dorm room, stumbled around, knocked some shit over, woke everyone up, hissed an apology, and crawled into my bunk to try to sleep. The sunlight seared through the cracks in the blinds. After an hour I realized this was totally futile.

I got up and returned to the KEX living room, this large but cozy space with a bar, tables, and some old-fashioned chairs that looked like they were plucked from a garage sale. I set up my iPad and wireless keyboard, grabbed some coffee from the bar (intended for people waking up for 7 a.m. flights) and hammered out a blog post for my employer, RedEye, a daily newspaper in Chicago.

### Blogging From Iceland a Spotty Proposition

OK, Off the Markley readers, let me apologize for my spotty blogging of the last week. Like I've been saying for a few weeks now, I'm going to Iceland. And now I'm in Iceland. Whoa. So here's the deal: Rather than dragging my laptop across glaciers and shit, I'm out here with just an iPad. And not even an iPad 2—we're talking an iPad 1, which is like having a Remington typewriter or Gutenberg printing press. I'm not even sure I know how to use my iPad for anything other than checking NBA playoff scores and watching Netflix.

All this to say, the frequency of my posts for the next two weeks will be subject to 1) how well I can figure out the Trib's P2P platform on this thing, since it looks kind of weird and for some reason the toolbar has vanished and I don't know how to link to anything 2) hostel Internet access and 3) the likelihood that me and my friends Bojo and Trin will meet a gaggle of Icelandic princesses who want us to hang out on their North Sea luxury yachtland (that's an island made out of a yacht).

So all I can really say is that I couldn't sleep; there was some Eurotrash douche bag sleeping in my bed in my 10-bed hostel room, and now I'm writing this while looking out over a bay cupped in the palm of low snow-capped mountains with spikes of golden morning light cutting through the slate-gray clouds overhead—otherwise known as an image I can't share with you because I don't know how to upload pictures from my camera to this iPad (I believe there's some cordage I'm missing).

What I'm saying, guys, is I'll do my best, I really will, but I suggest keeping an eye on this page, Facebook, Twitter, and possibly Icelandic social gossip columns in case those princesses pan out.

By noon that day I still hadn't bothered to try to sleep and instead found Bojo and Trin for breakfast. We spent the rest of the day wandering the city, which consists of one main drag with a lot of shops, bars, restaurants, and one enormous church on a hill towering over everything else. I won't bore you with a lot of description here except to say that Reykjavík is not any city you're used to. It is compact—tightly spaced in that European way where the streets in the city center are all slender enough to fool you into thinking they're sidewalks. The city kind of rests on a slope flowing downward from the church and bottoming out in a square near City Hall, which overlooks a picturesque little pond. I kept thinking my hometown of Mount Vernon, Ohio, generally felt about as grand as this. There was an enormous amount of graffiti in Reykjavík, which probably constitutes most of their street crime, but what didn't dawn on me until later was how little trash there was. You practically had to search for the litter. A coastal city, it looks out over the port and those low mountains along the opposite coast. This brought in a cool breeze that seemed to keep the city at exactly 55 degrees Fahrenheit during the day and about 45 at night.

**[And yes, I'll be exclusively using illogical American imperial measurements because I know how long a king's foot is, but haven't the foggiest as to how many meters I can run.]**

We wandered by City Hall, the pond, and back up to a bookstore to search for a movie. We were trying to find a copy of the film *Gnarr*, a documentary about Reykjavík's comedian mayor, because I'd just learned that day that he'd be granting me an interview the next week.

No one in Reykjavík had a copy of the film with English subtitles, which seemed impossible. We went into a video store (I'd discovered the previous night during my insomnia that Iceland has yet to learn about the existence of Netflix), and while we didn't find an English version of *Gnarr*, we did end up in an extensive conversation with the proprietor of the video and DVD establishment. This avuncular old man had the bug-eyes of Rodney Dangerfield and a lot of advice for us on how to approach Icelandic women (much, much more on this guy later).

Our last stop was the church, towering over the rest of Reykjavík from its perch on the highest hill. According to a totally not-thorough skimming of possibly the wrong Wikipedia page, the church is called "Hallgrímskirkja," (which is why I will be referring to it as "the church"). Construction began in 1937 but was not completed until 1986, which is totally bewildering and makes you wonder if the architect and construction workers were putting up a stone per day. One imagines the City Council hemming and hawing before saying, "Hey, I know Rome wasn't built in a day, but the idiom they'll make about Reykjavík is going to be pretty cruel if you guys don't get the fuck to work."

The design appears like a ripple of milky water cascading up to the bell tower, inspired by Iceland's basalt lava flows. It looks over a small plaza and a statue of Leif Ericson with his foot propped up, looking all manly and conquery and rapey. This statue was actually a gift from the United States.

**[You're welcome, Iceland. We'll call it even on inspiring your financial meltdown.]**

Inside, Trin, Bojo and I ascended to the bell tower without paying—not because we are bad people, but because the elevator was unguarded, a ticket 800 krónur, and if this was all some kind of social science experiment about trust, we were fine with failing and saving the six bucks.

"We're like *Ocean's Eleven* here," I noted. "Conned our way into Reykjavík's most heavily guarded church."

"You just wrote the screenplay to *Ocean's Fourteen*." said Bojo.

"Who am I?" asked Trin.

"Clooney. I'm Pitt, and Bojo's Damon. It only makes sense."

The view from the open-air tower was pretty spectacular, and you could see all the way past Reykjavík's outlying suburbs where the open country waited—the square, modular apartments of the city looking like a tidy Lego display. Downstairs, Trin took about 15 pictures of the enormous organ, which looked like a goddamn Transformer, all folded up and silver and gleaming with whatever organ-cleaning solution they use for such purposes.

"That is one enormous organ," I said to Bojo. "I'm not sure I've ever seen a bigger organ than that. You've seen a lot of organs, right, man? How big is this organ in comparison? Is it a massive organ or just a pretty big one?"

"Dude, c'mon, don't make dick jokes in a church," he said, trying to get away from me while I followed behind him loudly wondering how they fit such an enormous organ through a doorway.

## Icelandic Women

Because we were going out that night, I went back to the hostel and tried to get any possible sleep whatsoever to add to my four hours from three days ago (or whatever). Even with the sun scorching through the window, reflecting off of the blindingly white sheets and pillows of 10 hostel beds, I managed to get two. In multibed hostel rooms there are always travelers on strange schedules trying to sleep at weird times, and there was a girl on the bed above mine sleeping in nothing but a bra and underwear, which wasn't helping anything at all because I hadn't had a chance to touch myself since I last slept on my own mattress in Chicago (way too much on this later).

[In fact, I'm sad to say a large part of the philosophical ruminations of this tome will be about how hard it is to masturbate while traveling abroad.]

Yet add those two hours I did, bringing the total to six. When I found Bojo again, it turned out he'd bumped into two guys who'd gone to college with us. The short story is that both Bojo and I went to Miami University (In Ohio! In fucking Ohio, not Florida!), and though we were neighbors for two years, we did not know each other until we both lived in Chicago and met through a mutual friend.

Blake and Michael, also Miami alum, were also in Iceland for an extended stay, so we decided to join forces. It led to point three of my blog post "Things I Learned from 1.5 Nights in Reykjavík":

> 3) Guys from Miami University-parentheses-Ohio are omnipresent. We arrived at the KEX Hostel and Bojo literally bumped into a guy from his engineering program back in school. He was traveling with another Miami alum, so there were the five of us—four Miami grads— trying to explain to the Icelanders that this was all just a random coincidence.

We wolfed down dinner at a delicious, cheap Thai place called Noodle Station that would later become a staple dinner of the trip. I guess that falls under:

**Iceland Travel Tip #33:** Noodle Station is awesome and about the cheapest, most filling meal you're going to find in a city that costs a fortune, which brings me to point five of "Things I Learned":

> 5) Everything in Iceland costs a fortune. Even with a financial crisis, even with a highly devalued currency, this town has us bleeding money. A beer, it seems, is about the equivalent of $6 to $8, and this is just for the pisswater Euro equivalent of Bud. Of course, since I have no conception of what I'm spending (a thousand krónur here, two thousand there—every time I pay for a sandwich I feel like a Zimbabwean Deputy Secretary of Extraction or something), I'm simply not paying attention.

The point is Bojo, Trin, myself, and these two new American guys, Blake and Michael, hit the town on a Tuesday night to see what was what. We tried a bar called Lebowski, explicitly themed after the Jeff Bridges/Coen brothers cult masterpiece (what this translates into aesthetically is a bowling alley-themed, Playboy-spangled retro hell), but it was dead so we moved on to a bar called, I think, Vegamót, which we pronounced "Vej-uh-mot." We were not shocked to later learn that this was incorrect.

Here is why Iceland is awesome: We had barely managed to order from the bar when several very attractive young women arrived and sat down at the table beside ours. In America, this table of women would be out of bounds. You would never talk to them because they were very pretty, and you are a guy who respects women with rejection-ready physicality. Yet within nanoseconds of eye contact, these girls were offering to join the tables together.

For our purposes the three characters that will become important are:

Dóra: short, blond, extremely pretty in an Elvin way ("She was a-Dóra-ble," Bojo would say, to his great discredit).

Bryndís: medium-height, dark-haired, heaving, romance novel chest, talkative, extremely pretty in a vampiric way.

Arna: tall, darkly redheaded, freckled, slender, demur, extremely pretty in a sorceress way.

It turned out Dóra, Bryndís, and Arna were all flight attendants for Icelandair (go figure), and we went about explaining our occupations, why we'd traveled to Iceland, and what we planned to do while there. I told them how I planned to interview their mayor, Jón Gnarr.

"What do you think of him?" Trin asked.

"Oh, he is a joke," said Dóra. "It was very funny while he was running, but he will have his four years, and then they will get someone new."

"I have a question," I said. "We heard that the majority of the Icelandic believe in elves."

"Yes," said Bryndís. "That's true."

"So, do you?"

"No, I don't believe in them," said Dóra.

"It's like a very—how do you say?—a very popular thing to think, but no, not many people actually believe that," said Bryndís.

It turns out that while the Icelandic, like other Nordic peoples, are some of the least likely to believe in a magic man in the sky who holds the fate of the world in his invisible hands, they are far more likely, by a long shot, to believe in elves, trolls, and other "hidden people" who fall under the blanket term of *huldufólk*. A 2007 poll found that while only 8 percent believed in hidden people outright, 54 percent refuse to deny the existence of the creatures.

"What about you?" I asked Arna.

She sipped her drink delicately, and I could tell I'd found one of the 54 percent.

"It's not that I believe in them, but there are things that go unexplained," she said.

"Arna's mother gives tours," Bryndís volunteered.

"Really?" I asked.

"Yes," said Arna. "She gives tours of where the elves—the hidden people—are supposed to live."

"Where?"

"Not far from here. About 15 minutes outside the city. A place called Hafnarfjörður."

I looked at Bojo and Trin. "We should totally do that."

Arna agreed to send me the information on Facebook.

From there, the conversation turned to sex (as it usually does when there are a bunch of people sitting around who'd like to have it). The girls explained that Icelandic women were not what we were used to. Bryndís was particularly vociferous on this point.

"You Americans, you expect you must take the girls out on dates—what is a date? Why do I want to sit and talk to you? What are you saying that is interesting? Nothing. You are stupid. If I want sex from you, I will take it. That's what Icelandic women think."

We crowded around the table and listened to Bryndís expound.

"Oh, and you Americans have babies and so then you get married? Why would you do that? So you have a baby, so what? What does that mean you have to be around that person all the time?"

Dóra's eyes appeared to be flitting between Trin and I, although that was probably my wishful thinking. I was actually most interested in talking to Arna, who just gave off a cool, intelligent flare. I'm always a sucker for the girl who appears least interested in me.

"You will do great," said Bryndís. "Icelandic girls love Americans. You just go up to them and be bold. It is so easy. You'd have to be really stupid to not have sex with Icelandic girls. You just go to the bar, B5, that's where all the skinny girls are. They are like models, like sticks, and you just go up to them and start talking and tell them you're a writer or you're an engineer or whatever, and they will have sex with you. You'll have so much sex."

The five of us threw a bunch of raised eyebrows at each other.

"We don't have prostitutes in Iceland. Look around!" Bryndís cried. "There are no prostitutes anywhere. No ladies in the skimpy clothings going, 'Hey baby, you wanna ride?' We don't need prostitutes because you can just get it for free!"

What Bryndís said actually has a pretty important cultural context. For much of human history women have lived under the horrific thumb of men, subjected to all kinds of mistreatment, torture, and outright murder. Misogyny abounds in the developing world, but it turns out that when women become fully empowered and their numbers are not artificially lowered by men they naturally outnumber men by a slight margin. They use contraception, and the birth rate remains low. In turn, promiscuity increas-es and—at least this is my hypothesis—the men become bigger D-bags because they realize there are more women around, and they are suddenly a more valuable commodity. I firmly believe this will happen all over the world eventually: Women will attain most of the economic and political power while men will be lazy welfare recipients perpetually rejoicing that it's so easy to get laid.

**[Until the women scientists invent the third sex, which will basically be Women with a Magnificent Penis, which will be a dark day for us guys indeed.]**

At some point the group decided to make a move from Ve-gamót to another bar called Prikið (which we pronounced "Pree-kid" but which Icelanders call "Pree-kith" because there's this fun-ny Icelandic letter that looks like the out-of-wedlock child of a "P" and "D" and apparently is pronounced with a "th" sound). Prikið would become our go-to bar in Reykjavík: A simple cafe by day-time that morphs into a badass neighborhood bar at night. There was a female DJ there with a CD book that looked exactly like mine from senior year of high school—just endless, awesome old-school rap. Tupac, Biggie, Outkast, early Jay-Z, Big-fucking-Pun, for Christ's sake! It was almost too awesome to bear. Prikið also had these retro lights hanging from the ceiling that patrons were encouraged to grab and hurl around in fits of '90s hip-hop rapture. The girls danced, and Bojo ordered a round of beers for everyone, ignoring my eye-warnings of "Dude, that's going to cost a fortune." Then Trin ordered shots for everyone.

He asked the girls for a recommendation, and we ended up with nine shots of this murky, anonymous black liquid.

"Skál!" we all said.

["Skál" obviously being the word for "cheers". This is one of the few words I ever manage to learn in any country in which I travel ("Prost!" "Salud!" "Cin Cin!"). The only other word I became familiar with in Iceland was "Takk," which means "Thank you" and can be useful in all situations where you want someone to say something completely incomprehensible back to you.]

Which brings me to the fourth point of "Things I Learned":

4) There is some shot that a bunch of girls got us to buy, which may be the worst alcoholic liquid I've ever tried to get past my uvula, including isopropyl. This thing was like Jaeger that had run through the sphincter of a swine with colorectal cancer. It was a licorice, maple-syrup-type, soy sauce concoction that I wanted to spit back into the shot glass. Trin, who is supposed to be on a seven-month trip and for whom this was day three, bought 10 of them. Good luck keeping that pace up, buddy.

When Prikið kicked us out at 1 a.m., the girls invited us back to one of their apartments for an after-party. We really should have looked at the situation and debated this more—especially me. I was going on six hours of sleep in the last two days, was drunk, and saw that some Icelandic D-bag had attached himself to our group, which threatened to disrupt all potential chemistry and tilt the guy-to-girl ratio precariously in the wrong direction.

This guy, apparently a pilot for Icelandair, had latched onto our group at Vegamót and followed us to Prikið. He was tall and blond with that terrible Icelandic haircut where it's shaved on the sides and parted just below the crown of the skull. Bryndís also informed me that upon spotting Bojo and Trin, this guy said to Dóra, "What happened, did Greece throw up in here?"

**[OK, so I actually found that pretty hilarious. Good one, Icelandair pilot.]**

But now this Icelandic D-bag had infiltrated our group, and worse, appeared to be wooing Dóra away from our five-way American clutches. Trin was especially distressed because he really did appear on the path to touching at least one of Dóra's boobs.

"Well," I said to Blake, Michael, and Bojo. "We don't really have a choice. We're in Iceland and hot Icelandic girls have invited us back to an apartment to drink more. We have to play this out."

The cab ride took us to an apartment complex on the outskirts of the city where my fears were born out. Dóra was getting the full-court press from Icelandic pilot-guy,

**[Who, it turned out, was divorced and had two kids. I mean—wha? He looked like he was twenty-six! Let me tell you something, Icelandic people: When you're divorced with two kids in America, you do not get to go out and bang hot, blond Elvin girls! Being divorced means you're a sad, pitiful loser-dud who eats peanut butter and jelly sandwiches off of his pale beer gut and spends all his time wallowing in the abject failure of his life and certainty that his kids will grow up to hate and resent him—as God intended!]**

Arna was out on the small balcony chain-smoking cigarettes and looking incredibly vexed, and I had somehow managed to involve myself in a political debate with Bryndís. I forget how it started, but this exchange was in there:

"You Americans, you come over here; you know nothing about the world!" she complained.

"I don't disagree," I said.

"In school, we don't just learn about Iceland; we have to learn about Africa and Europe and the United States, so we know about all of these places and Americans never know anything that happened outside of America."

"Look, you're not going to get me to disagree that Americans are entitled, myopic dunces," I told her, understanding that I'd much rather be staring at her chest than trying to score rhetorical points in a geo-political debate. Unfortunately, I'm incapable of walking away from an argument when I feel I have a point to make. "I'll grant you that. I'll grant you all of that. But that doesn't mean, at the same time, that Iceland is not a place of vast privilege in proportion to the rest of the world."

"What privilege?" she cried. "What privilege are you talking about?"

"The very fact that you have the luxury of going out with your friends and wearing pretty clothes and drinking alcohol—"

"These shoes!" she shouted, missing my point. "These shoes I got for discount! For very discount!"

And then we were just talking over each other.

"But that doesn't negate the fact that the abundance that first-world countries enjoy—like Iceland—"

"What languages does an American ever know? I know four languages! All Icelandic, we know many languages. Americans can't even speak English!"

"—is only made possible by the relative poverty of the rest of the world, that there really isn't enough to go around if we all want to live these high-consumption, energy-intensive lifest—"

"Americans don't even know how to find Iceland on the map!"

So that was fun. By the time Bryndís and I had brought the room's conversation to a halt, the Icelandic D-bag who insulted my friends had absconded with Dóra. We began to see that we'd overstayed our welcome. The math just never added up. It was one of those situations where the sheer volume of penis in the room wrung all the fun out of it. We called a cab and made the trudge back to our hostel.

"You know, for girls who spent about an hour telling us how stupid we would be if we couldn't get laid in Iceland, that sure didn't go so well," noted Bojo.

"Maybe that was their joke," wondered Trin. "Maybe that's the joke they'll all play."

I crawled into bed at 4 a.m. We had to be up by 8 a.m. to pick up our rental car. *Ten hours of sleep in the first 72*, I thought. Not a bad start.

When I closed my eyes, I dreamt of Kiefer Sutherland having a drunken fistfight with Big Pun in Heaven.

# THREE

## The Context

It's impossible to talk about Iceland without providing the context of what happened here four years prior to my arrival. Iceland was at the absolute zenith of the credit bubble that nearly sank the world in 2008.

I know. This is going to suck because it will involve learning. It may also suck because instead of awesome stories about Kiefer Sutherland getting his rocks off by yelling at small men, you'll have to listen to my Minskyite rantings about how turning financial innovation into the bedrock of your economy will inevitably bring with it greed, corruption, crisis, and misery—otherwise known as "reality." However, just hold on to your bucket seats, and I promise we'll get back to tales of road-trip masturbation in no time.

At the start of the new millennium, Iceland's free market-obsessed Independence Party decided it would be a good idea to privatize the banking sector and allow it free rein to build the country's wealth. Power ended up in the hands of a few wealthy businessmen who hired bankers with little to no experience in international banking. These bankers began issuing bonds by the vat-load. As the financial writer Michael Lewis put it, "Basically fishermen were walking off their boats into banking jobs." Foreign investors gobbled that shit up, though, because Iceland had no history of instability. As a result, money flowed into Iceland and the banks helped investors purchase stakes in every half-witted business plan; the housing market soared in value, cars—and everyone knows a car depreciates the second you drive it off the lot—could be sold used for more than their original value. The stock market skyrocketed 900 percent between 2002 and 2008. Icelandic Gordon Gekkos went hoovering up international credit, especially from Britain and Denmark, as the average family saw its wealth rocket up by 45 percent. People were walking into Porsche dealerships, applying for 100 percent loans with 60 to 70 percent of the loan in a foreign currency instead of krónur.

What happened in Iceland mirrors America in some ways and is dissimilar in others. One place, however, where the parallel is striking is the brain drain Big Finance created. During the aughts, basically everyone in the country went into banking. If you look at the history of financial crises, one striking similarity they all share is the run up to the bubble and the focus on finance within the larger economy leads to a vacuuming up of a disproportionate amount of young talent and ingenuity into the financial sector. Smart people don't spend their time on the next great innovation; instead they focus on attempting to create money out of money. Students at the University of Iceland went from taking courses in the economics of fishing to studying complicated investment instruments and option-pricing models. It's happened over and over again for centuries. As economists Carmen Reinhart and Kenneth

Rogoff put it in their book *This Time is Different: Eight Centuries of Financial Folly*, the mantra is always, "This time is different."

But it never is, and it wasn't in Iceland.

At the height of the splurge, assets held by Icelandic banks were worth 744 percent of the country's gross domestic product. Foreign money provided most of the fire's fuel, and when those bonds suddenly came due during the global financial crisis, banks had nothing to back up this insanity. From there it was your standard bank run, with foreign depositors rushing to yank their money out of Icelandic banks and a government that didn't have the capability of a TARP-style plan to bail them out. The banks failed. With debt 850 percent of GDP, all the government could do was guarantee people's basic savings accounts. Yet with so much money wrapped up in investment funds and other vehicles that people always assume are safe bets (because bankers always tell you it's a safe bet), many in the country lost huge sums of money. They lost their homes, cars, and found themselves drowning in debt because during the boom years it was easy to get foreign currency loans. Well, when your currency plummets and you owe a bunch of euros that are suddenly much more expensive, the payments you have to make on your mortgage or car loan suddenly explode. People burned their cars for the insurance. They withdrew huge amounts of worthless krónur. They hoarded food. At one point, Iceland's krónur was rated above only the currencies of Zimbabwe and Turkmenistan. A weak currency hurts an island nation that has to import so much—consumer prices rose 34 percent as a result. Ten percent tax increases took hold and interest rates hit 18 percent to combat inflation. Unemployment spiked to 9 percent, a near-unthinkable number for a country that has had labor shortages for half a century.

Of course, the same type of cheerleaders you see on CNBC or channeling money from Wall Street to American political parties led the Icelandic boom. In a 2005 talk in London, Ólafur Ragnar Grímsson, the president of Iceland, said, "We are succeeding because we are different, and our track record should inspire the business establishment in other countries to re-examine their previous beliefs and norms . . . You ain't seen nothing yet."

Prophecies of creating wealth from thin air is the oldest fairy tale with the most predictable and grimmest of endings. The great Icelandic novelist Halldór Laxness wrote as far back as 1946:

> It had likewise been nothing uncommon for people thus denied sustenance to die of starvation, but such a fate, surely, was infinitely preferable to being ensnared by the banks, as people are nowadays, for at least they had lived like independent men, at least they had died of hunger like free people. The mistake lies in assuming that the helping hand proffered by the banks is as reliable as it is seductive, when in actual fact the banks may be relied upon only by those few exceptionally great men who can afford to owe anything from one to five million.

They called it the *Hrun*, or downfall. Yet when the crash came, Iceland served as a case study for what to do right in the wake of a financial crisis. For all the vituperative invective the common Icelander hurled at the government over the course of our time in the country, the powers that be actually got it right where much of Europe got it totally wrong. First of all, Iceland got a 6 billion euro rescue from the International Monetary Fund and some of its fellow Nordic countries. Rather than forcing austerity on its citizens while bailing out financial institutions, it let the banks go bust and reinforced its social safety net. There was pain, but not nearly as much as the countries that would attempt to reinvigorate their economies by slashing programs and spending. Instead they allowed their currency to depreciate, repudiated their debt, and enforced capital controls—otherwise known as the exact opposite of European Central Bank and Republican Party doctrine. Iceland emerged from recession in December of 2010 with 2.3 percent growth. By the time we visited, the country's GDP was back to where it was just before 2007, and without the inflated banking sector. Pain remains and the country must now pivot. Its people— at one point the wealthiest per capita in the world—must figure out how they will recover from their society-rattling *Hrun*.

Over the course of my stay in the country, I'd ask Icelanders how they felt about their homeland's catastrophic financial implosion. The word I heard most often was "reflection."

Later, you'll read about an elf tour we took in Hafnarfjörður with Arna's mother, a woman named Sibba Karlsdottir. Following a guided viewing of Elvin hangouts and dwarf baths, I asked Sibba to tell me about the crisis, and what she said not only summarized the Icelandic view of the downfall but told you everything you needed to know about what we didn't do in the United States.

"I did what everyone did," she said. "I took cash out, I bought food. It was panic. And after it was very hard. People lost their houses, their cars. But it was a time for a lot of reflection. I think a lot of people looked at themselves and took an appraisal. What do I want from life? What is it that makes for happiness? Is it a big house and many nice cars? Is it just nice things? I don't know the answer, but I think that many people came to a conclusion about this."

From my limited time in the country, I heard this sentiment repeated during our travels: the *Hrun* was a time to reassess. To remind each other what was important. In America, all you ever seemed to hear from any side of the political spectrum were ideas about how to get the party going again, how to re-create the materialism of the bubble years, which many Americans simply consider normality.

Not that this is meant as, "Hey, I met these funny little island folk, who taught me the meaning of life!" Not at all. But just the fact that so many Icelanders of disparate perspectives used the word "reflection" to describe their society-wide introspection has often made me yearn for the possibilities of a similar reaction and reflection from my own homeland.

***An Icelandic Roadtrip***

*Illustration © SiggaRún, 2013*

# FOUR

# The Road Trip Begins

*Hey!!! Dont be telling everyone what I told you! hahaha and buy the way its not called Jaeger, it was GAJOL from Denmark!!! We have a better one called Topas and Opal and it doesnt taste like Soya Sauce haha*

—Bryndís, on my Facebook wall, after reading my blog post.

In an effort to encourage tourism, Iceland has made it cheap and easy to rent a car and travel the country. They drive on the same side of the road as us, so there's not the terror factor of British-style driving, but as our car rental guy warned us, make sure you get the gravel insurance, for reasons that will be explained.

Any road trip with friends becomes a fractured, disjointed amalgamation of lost moments, inside jokes, long silences, the same songs returned to the stereo speakers again and again, and strange tangents followed as far as logic or illogic will allow. It's impossible to reproduce a road trip sequentially in a way that lends it the same kind of meaning you felt during the drive. I'll do my best to remain faithful to the spirit of that week-plus we spent on the highways and byways of Iceland. To keep you visually stimulated, it will contain a lot of bolding, italicizing, indenting, and even some bullet points because I'm a crazy motherfucker like that.

## Ellldbooorg!

We'd only been out of Reykjavík for a little over an hour, cruising north and then curving to the west to drive around Snæfellsnes, Iceland's almost-westernmost peninsula, when Trin had us make our first stop of the trip.

Trin had found some kind of traveler's itinerary for sights to visit while driving around Iceland, and the first stop on that plan was a place called the Eldborg Crater, which is a "spatter cone" along a short volcanic rift.

**[Incidentally, a "spatter cone" would also be Bojo's signature move if he ever stars in pornography.]**

Eldborg is part of the beautifully named volcanic system Ljó-sufjöl, which means "the mountains of the light." Recognizing that the name "Eldborg" really should belong to a character from *Game of Thrones* or *Harry Potter*, I quickly took to calling the formation, "*Elllldbooorg!*" in as Voldemort a voice as I could manage. Eldborg had the last laugh, however, because our short hike to the rim involved almost more than we'd bargained for. Keep in mind, we were all still pretty hung over from the "GAJOL!". I was running on those 10 hours of sleep in the previous 72, and the 2½ kilometer hike (yeah, I have no conception of how far that is either) ended with a short but taxing scramble up the rim of the crater where you had to kind of pull yourself up the chain-link railing driven into the rock. After that, there was no railing to speak of, and we stared down over the crater's edge, which essentially had a cliff face on either side.

"Wow, that's really no joke," said Trin, looking down at the drop-off into the crater's lichen-covered interior.

A cold wind blew, freezing the sweat to my skin and ripping off Bojo's hat, so that he had to hop over the chains that clearly delineated the safe part of the crater's rim from the not-at-all-safe part. It's moments like this when I'm glad I'd talked myself out of having vertigo when I was a kid by just jumping off every tall thing a 12-year-old could find in Knox County, Ohio.

On the way back down, we waited until we were hidden amongst the shrub-draped lava field and all peed into the schizophrenic wind.

**Iceland Travel Tip #14:** There are no rest stops in Iceland, but that's OK because you can pee almost anywhere (if you're a guy—and really, if you're a girl, too). I peed at just about every place we stopped, from side-of-the-highway attractions to awe-inspiring geological formations such as the place where the Eurasian and North American tectonic plates meet. I never understand people who find peeing in nature uncouth. Where do they think the pee ends up when you flush it?

"Damnit!" I said, zipping up my fly.

"What's up, man?" Trin asked, dropping back to walk beside me.

"You know when you think you're done pissing, and you put your dick back in and then that last little jet comes out? That just happened to me."

"Ah, I hate that."

"I know. Now I have pee all over my legs and it's cold."

"We're getting old," said Bojo over his shoulder. "Our urethras don't work like they used to. The muscle's starting to get worn out."

"You'd think science would be on that," I said.

"Does that mean when we're like 50 we'll just be pissing down the side of our legs all the time?" wondered Trin.

"'What'd you do in Iceland, Steve?' 'Oh, nothing much, Grandma. Went to the Eldborg Crater and talked with my buddies about how our dicks don't work right anymore. The *yoooj*, as they say.'"

## Snuffelufegus and the Icelandic Sagas

As you've probably noticed by now, the Icelandic language takes all the incomprehensibility of your basic Nordic language, stirs in a Gaelic influence, adds a dash of inbred-Viking ornery, and pretty soon you have the most cumbersome, inexplicable, unpronounceable words that still use an alphabet you recognize. While Bojo drove, Trin and I spent our time figuring out where to go next, which involved him and I trying to read Icelandic town and location names. We developed a system where we just came up with the closest approximation we could manage and Anglicized whatever we were looking for.

"Okay," said Trin. "When we round the end of the peninsula, we should be able to see Snuffelufegus."

Snuffelufegus being the glacier Snæfellsjökull, which means "snow-fells glacier." Snuffelufegus retains much literary fame: in Jules Verne's classic *A Journey to the Center of the Earth*, it's where Professor Von Hardwigg (legendary Brendan Fraser role alert!) and his nephew Alex find the passage down a volcano tube that begins their quest. Snuffelufegus is actually one of Iceland's smaller glaciers, but in driving by and seeing the way the pure, driven white of the ice seemed to ooze a cold, pale steam that gathered in a cloud above the mighty ice mass, I grew excited for the other glacial behemoths we'd see in the days to come.

"How far is it to Grundelford?" asked Bojo.

"Grundelford" was our name for the town of Grundarfjörður because it's easier to pronounce the American word meaning "the nice little piece of flesh between the balls and asshole" than however you say a word that has an "o" with a little "x" over it.

We were also crossing historical paths with one of Iceland's most infamous mythic heroes, Grettir the Strong. The most important component of Iceland's literary tradition is a series of stories written by anonymous authors from roughly 1200 to 1400. Together they comprise the doorstop tome of *The Iceland Sagas*, and they serve as the mytho-historical foundation of a wind-driven, hardscrabble land not far removed from an unruly past teeming with ghosts and violence and mystery. The Sagas also have a surprisingly robust influence on the Western canon, including legendary director John Huston, who admits to lifting many of his plots straight from the Icelandic texts.

Grettir is one of the Sagas' most redolent personalities: a brawling, womanizing sinner—part Robin Hood, part Paul

Bunyan, part Charlie Sheen. He's based on an actual outlaw named Grettir Ásmundarson, who died in 1050 c.e., according to census records. The Saga of Grettir describes its hero spending most of his time getting banished from different lands, pissing off the wealthy and powerful while bedding their daughters, battling evil spirits and trolls, jacking travelers' horses at sword-point, and generally being a badass motherfucker. A typical morning for Grettir would be to argue "with a neighbor boy named Skeggi; Skeggi seized his axe and struck at Grettir, who grabbed the shaft of the axe and wrenched it free. Then Grettir struck Skeggi with the same axe, through to his brain."

The Sagas mostly consist of horrific acts of violence interrupted every once in a while with quips of the darkest gallows humor. So, Anglo-Saxon literary tradition, thanks for all those sleep-inducing Bible translations, you stupid, boring fuckers.

## The Town Pool Situation

By the time we arrived in Grundelford, we were starving and exhausted. From my subsequent RedEye blog post:

> In the summer here the sun basically never sets. Sometime around 1 a.m. it looks like a typical Midwestern dusk and then an hour later like a typical dawn, but that's about it. Permanent daylight tricks my biological clock apparently, and it tricks it good—mostly because my body still thinks it's seven years old.
>
> "No, no, no!" says my biological clock. "What are you doing? It's still light-time out! Let's play. Take off your

shirt, rub mud on your face, and pretend you're King Kong! Then let's get into Dad's liquor cabinet!"

We spent our day of imminent exhaustion rolling along in our rental car, turning around a lot because Iceland only has six roads and therefore their roadmaps are written kind of like, "Yeah, hmm, well, this one kinda goes here, and this little gravel one kind of goes this way, and I don't know, you'll figure it out . . . ", listening to Bon Iver's "Holocene" and trudging up the rims of extinct volcanoes on wind-battered plains . . .

We made our way to a lava field where we found a small church and a cemetery overlooking the peninsula's southern coast. The Icelandic, it seems, are very fond of building churches in totally inaccessible rural fields, fjord cliff faces, and just splat in the middle of glaciers. They probably know Americans like it that way for our Bon Iver videos.

Too tired to find a grocery store, we stopped at the first and only restaurant we spotted in the town of 900 people. Basically, all they had was pizza.

"I'm so glad we get to sample all of this traditional Icelandic food," said Trin, looking over the menu. "Pizza, burgers, and even cheeseburgers!"

"It's probably because they got tired of eating sheep meat," I told him. "Someone came over here with a pizza and the Vikings all dropped their spit-cooked sheep and said, 'Whoa, buddy, lemme getta fucking loada that!'"

**[Icelandic delicacies actually do include some rather unbelievable fare that didn't exactly sound appetizing to an American's palate.**

The ultra-famous one is *hakarl,* which is when you take a Greenland shark, cut off its head, bury it in the ground with stones on top pressing the fluids out of the body for six to twelve weeks and then hang it out to dry for a few months. It apparently tastes like ammonia and most people gag when they try to eat it. Then there's *reykur lax,* which is salmon smoked over sheep dung. Finally, the king daddy comes in the form of the midwinter feast known as Þorramatur. Dishes include boiled sheep's heads, a pudding made from sheep liver, sheep's loins cured in lactic acid, seal flippers, and boiled ram's testicles. Most of these traditional food items tell you about the remarkable scarcity of resources Icelandic settlers faced over the centuries, not to mention their remarkable resilience and inventiveness in the face of such dietary uncertainty. Given my deep respect for this tradition, one might think I sampled all of these treats that we heard of along our journey. However, it turns out I do not give a sweet syrupy fuck about being the next Anthony Bourdain and tried nothing.]

After our meal we asked about how to get to our hostel.

"About 800 kilooo-meters down these roads and turn right at the pool," the waitress told us.

Leaving the restaurant, Bojo said, "That's the second time someone's given us directions based on a swimming pool."

On our way to the hostel, we saw not one, not two, but three signs pointing toward the town pool. This was our first encounter with the Icelandic's utter obsession with swimming pools. What did I learn about Icelandic culture? These beautiful, blond-haired people love the shit out of swimming pools. They are totally obsessed with their swimming pools the way Americans are obsessed with Kardashians. In every town we traveled to after that, I couldn't help but notice how many people directed us to specific locations using the town swimming pool as a landmark ("Yes, just go past the pool . . ." "If you take a left at the pool . . ." "Go to the swimming pool, and then travel 450 kilometers to the north . . ."). Nor could I escape the sheer volume of taxpayer money that went to funding signs that pointed in the direction of the pool. This was doubly odd because most Icelandic towns other than Reykjavík have populations of less than 1,000 people and one main road, so you can basically jump real high and spot whatever it is you're looking for, yet the number of signs with the little swimmy stick-figure-guy doing laps in pointy waves seemed to outnumber the potential streets on which the pool could possibly lay.

At our hostel, I refused to pay the $9 for a sheet and blanket because I don't like having my comfort held hostage by Big Hostel and because I was on the verge of passing out from exhaustion anyway. We arrived in our five-bed room to discover that our two female roommates had decided to open both the windows, lowering the temperature to about 50 degrees. I closed the windows upon arriving, stepped out, and returned to discover both open again.

"Hey," I said to one of them. "Do you mind if we close the windows? It's freezing in here."

"Oh," she said. "We are hot. We live on the glacier, so this is very warm to us."

Of course. Of course you live on the glacier. How silly of me to think the people we were sharing a room with for one night wouldn't, obviously, be on a brief stay from their campground on the Snuffelufegus Glacier. Also, one of these women "staying on the glacier" was very evidently about eight months pregnant (we think Bojo did it).

**Inside Joke #6:** Bojo loves boats on land. This began the day after driving away from Grundelford when we were in the town of "Stykisham" (Stykkishólmur), which looks over to the Northwest fjords and has a weird new-agey church that looks like a rabbit impersonating the Sphinx. While driving around the coastal village, we spotted a beached boat tilting to its side in the sand. It looked long-abandoned and weathered, the paint washed away in huge chunks, a fishing shipwreck from an ancient storm perhaps. Bojo pointed it out and said, "That's cool. I really like that."

"Really like what?" I asked.

"Just the look of that boat. I just think it's really cool. It just looks really cool. I really like it."

"Whoa, Mike, I never knew you were this passionate about boats," said Trin from the backseat.

"But just boats on land," I added.

"I don't know," said Boj. "Something about it."

Thereafter, we took his comment on the pleasing aesthetic nature of a picturesque scene from a small fishing village and never let it go. Every time we saw any kind of water-vessel on land, we'd point it out. "Bojo, get your camera! It's your thing, man!"

"Boat on land! Boat on land!"

Or if we just saw a boat in the water: "Man, that boat would look great if it just had some goddamn land around it."

I guess you had to be there.

## Sad Corollary to Inside Joke #6

It turns out that one of the reasons there are so many beached boats lying around Iceland is because of a fishing quota system concocted by the Icelandic government. Keep in mind Iceland was a remarkably poor country until about a century ago when the first motorized boats made large-scale fishing possible, modestly boosting the average Icelander's income. Over the course of the next seventy-five years, Iceland became a nation of fisherman, but with stocks depleting, the government decided it needed to install a quota system to keep the fisheries from collapsing. On its face this was a good idea; overfishing is a common and severe problem all over the world. But the way the system worked was that fisherman were given quotas based on their current catch, and these quotas could be bought, sold, and compounded with no restriction, allowing the largest trawling companies to gather permits and force smaller fisherman out of business. Monopolies became entrenched interests, and the country's most valuable public resource became the private property of the elite. Twenty companies have come to dominate 70 percent of the national catch, and they exert enormous political power. Thus the boats of failed fisherman still sit abandoned in the small villages after they sold their quotas and left. Some of the permits still stuck in the windows apparently date back to the 1980s.

On the one hand, the quota system has allowed Icelandic fishing to become sustainable after near collapses of the cod stock in the '70s. On the other hand, a bunch of lucky fisherman who got the bulk of the free quotas in 1983 now run the industry, the so-called "Quota Kings." During the run-up to the *Hrun*, these guys borrowed money against their quotas and dipped into the banks' fancy array of new duplicitous financial products, which helped add gasoline to the stock market's blaze. The fishing companies' borrowing grew to the same size as the entire national budget. In other words, the quota system, which saved the country's most important industry, also created the huge wealth enclaves that helped bankrupt it.

The paradox being that Iceland's quota system served as a successful model for sustaining an overexploited resource, but its political and economic implications look just as ugly and destructive as the privatization of any commons. The government has since voted to return 15 percent of the quotas to the state by 2026—for explicit use by the people of Iceland, which they hope will act as a countervailing force to monopolies.

Meanwhile the European Union—with 90 percent of its seas overfished—watches and attempts to figure out a middle ground.

[**Hey Markley, if you make me learn one more fucking thing about privatized commons or fishing quotas or stock markets or some other bullshit learny-thing, you can shove this Iceland book straight up your ass.**"]

## The Highway Situation

The cheapest car we could rent was a silver Hyundai i20, a four-door Euro job that they don't even bother to sell in the States because it would threaten our collective masculinity. It got great gas mileage, barely had room for all of our bags in the little hatchback trunk, and came equipped with all the four-cylinder *oomph* of a donkey. We dubbed it the i-Twat.

The basic driving situation changed little over the course of our road trip. Bojo was the only one insured to drive, so he did most of it, though a few days into the trip, I insisted on a turn behind the wheel. I mostly sat shotgun, acting as navigator, while Trin stuck to the backseat, looking pretty and gazing pensively at scenery. Beside him, we kept backpacks, miscellaneous food, toilet paper, bottled water, a laptop, maps, and whatever other detritus we collected along the way. My entire life, I've become used to fighting my friends, younger sister, and all comers tooth-and-nail for shotgun, so I found it totally shocking when—the second time we loaded into the car after finishing our hike to *Elllldbooorg!*—I offered Trin shotgun and he declined.

"That's OK, man, I like the backseat. I like to look around. I feel like I've got my setup going pretty well back there."

Overjoyed because shotgun is the Holy Grail of passenger seats, and it just got abdicated to me for the rest of the trip, I told Trin I'd see him in hell.

**[Plus, everyone knows it's called "shotgun" because back in the old West the only guys who could sit in it had to have dicks as long as a shotgun. That's just history.]**

As it turned out, it's a pretty goddamn good thing I rode beside Bojo and acted as navigator. Let's just put it this way: You learn a lot about people when you travel with them. For instance, I long ago learned that I really like maps. I'm like a little 5-year-old who still thinks the Coca-Cola *Indiana Jones and the Last Crusade* promotional material that contains a small map with a dotted red line leading to different Coca-Cola products along a blob of unspecified land mass actually corresponds to stuff in real life. In other words, I like knowing where I am. I like being able to walk out of a building and orient myself immediately. Trin, I noticed quickly, would occasionally walk in the wrong direction to the sink after pissing in the toilet.

Once, when the three of us were leaving our place to get dinner, Trin first walked out of the door without his wallet (so Bojo grabbed it for him) and then upon reaching the street, immediately set off in the exact wrong direction.

"Yeah, you're going to do real well on your own for seven months," Bojo pointed out to him. "Right now you'd be wandering in the completely wrong direction without your wallet."

The point is our system worked. Trin was in charge of finding destinations, and I was in charge of getting us there.

"Bojo you drive and shut the fuck up, if you know what's good for you," said Trin.

"I just can't believe we've made it this far without Steve making a road-head joke," Bojo observed.

"Oh, you'd like that, wouldn't you?" I said, studying the map. "It all starts as a joke, and then, 'Hey, Steve, for real, I'm feeling sleepy. This is dangerous. There's only one thing that'll keep me awake, man.' I know your game, Bojo."

A piece of gravel whipped up from the road and cracked against the windshield.

"Guess that guy was right about the gravel protection," Bojo said.

The thing with Icelandic roads is this: There are only three kinds in the whole country. The first one on the map is red, which means a *paved road* and generally *not terrifying*. Generally. In

Iceland, guardrails are this extant luxury on par with potable water in Ethiopia. Every once in a while, we'd be driving up the side of a mountain and the drop-off down a cliff face to our immediate left would lead to butt-hole puckering that could turn coal into a diamond. Most "red" roads just had these reflective yellow plastic posts every few meters that I assumed were mostly for the winter when people had to drive with only two hours of daylight available. Two tight lanes lead you to slow down every time you pass a car coming the other way, and if it's a truck—which looked like ugly, snout-heavy monsters from the low seating of the i-Twat— you basically stop. Oh, and all the bridges are one lane and drivers from each direction take turns.

The second type of road is a dotted line on the map, which is *track*. You're not supposed to travel on track unless you have a four-wheel drive vehicle, and the entire country is replete with warnings about this. The rental car guy scolded us sternly; the emergency brochures in hostels all made a point of this, and even the video store clerk in Reykjavík offered unsolicited advice on the subject: "Many tourists, they walk on glaciers, fall through and die. Or they drive on rivers after all snow is melting and they get, uh, how you say? Washed away. You do not walk on glaciers or drive on rivers. You come back to my video store. Come back to Reykjavík and take home pretty girls."

Entrusted as the navigator, the scariest road I ever took us on is the third type, *maintained gravel*. In the States, we are used to having every road that sees any traffic at all paved. In Iceland they leave a great number of roads outside of the main highway (known as Highway 1) as gravel. For instance, there was no way to get from Stykkishólmur to our next destination without taking a gravel road. We realized too late how much dust the car kicked up, even going no faster than about 40 mph, and soon the interior of the car became covered in a thin coat of dust that would later turn up in our nostrils as boogers thicker and more chitinous than H.R. Geiger's *Alien*. These first gravel roads were some of the least spectacular of the drive. After spending the previous day cleaving between snow-capped mountains and the wild coast, we were suddenly in the midst of barren, rocky hills a color of brown so drab it was invented for the word.

## Erik's Store

The next stop after completing our loop around the peninsula was the farmhouse of Erik the Red (Eiríksstaðir, or "Erik's Store" as Trin and I negotiated). If you're not up to speed on your Viking history, a quick lesson: the Vikings came from the Scandinavian countries that today comprise Sweden, Denmark, Norway, etc. The nicest, most peaceful democratic-socialist countries on the planet used to be full of raping, murdering psychopaths who spent all their time raiding villages, burning people alive, cutting them apart in grotesque games of torturous barbarism, and generally being total assholes. They expanded westward, eventually establishing colonies on Iceland, Greenland, and even an attempt on the North American continent. It's true that they were the non-native "discoverers" of America well before Chrissy Columbus' grandfather was a glean in his pappy's balls, but they abandoned the experiment quickly because the natives did not like being murdered and decided to swing their weapons back, which the Vikings thought was just so not fair.

Even though many Vikings probably tried to colonize Greenland, Erik the Red gets the credit for its discovery. His son, Leif Ericson, became an even more renowned figure in Icelandic lore—sort of the Nordic George Washington—which just goes to show that it's only a very recent advent of human civilization that raping and stabbing everyone you meet should be viewed negatively.

Erik's Store lay beside a low-flow river in a farming valley. It's actually a replica of Erik the Red's home based on ruins discovered a few kilometers to the east back in 1997. We parked and took a few pictures of the exterior, a mud hut with a grass-coated exterior (no doubt held on with some kind of contemporary adhesive). It looked like a boil coming out of the hillside. Ducking through the entranceway, we found a small, ancient-replicated room with rows of wooden benches on either side, replica-tools of farming and dismemberment scattered about, and animal skins covering everything. A small fire probably feeding off a gas line cooked in a pit in the room's center, and sitting patiently on the bench watching was a woman dressed in, I assume, traditional female Viking garb. She looked at us, her eyes as wide as dinner plates.

"Hello," she said.

Is there anything more awkward than the historical re-enactor? I can never go to Colonial Williamsburg because I have no interest in some guy with a tri-cornered hat following me around and explaining how the Revolutionary Army ate beets and what tools they used to shovel the horse droppings. Historical re-enactors have a singular power to make the fascinating tale of human history seem dweeby and vaguely pedophilic. Luckily, there was a British couple occupying the woman's attention, but even as I tried to extract us from the situation before things got really awkward, I saw that Trin had lagged behind and was now listening, rapt, to the woman's laconic description of Viking life.

"Everyone lived in the same space," she said, her accented English dripping out of her mouth like slow honey. "The slaves ate and slept on that side and Erik the Red and his family slept here." She patted the bench where she sat. "All of them."

"That's very small!" declared the female half of the British couple. "How'd they all fit?"

"They slept sitting upright," she explained. The fire's light reflected in her SETI-dish sized eyes, and I wondered if she took painkillers during her shift just to make the time go more pleasantly. "They alternated directions. Vikings believed that if you lay down on your back your soul could escape more easily, and you'd die. So they all slept sitting up."

She was staring right at me in that way that makes you feel like you have to ask a question. "And this was supposedly the site where Erik the Red began his people's westward expansion. To Greenland and America," I said, unable to meet her glassy orbs.

"It is true," she said, hands on her lap, smile slight and flickering like the fire. "This area was likely the birthplace of Leif Ericson, but we also know that the Vikings landed in America. They've found tools and coins and other artifacts showing their presence. Would anyone like to try this on?"

She held up a metal Viking helmet, the one with the superfluous rectangle of metal extending over the nose.

"He would," I said, pointing to Bojo.

"Oh," said Bojo. "Uhh, good."

She handed him the helmet, and he put it on. Then she began draping animal skins over him. Bojo stood there grinning stupidly while Trin photographed him.

"These are going to be classic," said Trin. "Mike, you look fearsome."

"Do I look like I'd have slaves?" he asked. "Do I get a sword?"

The woman handed him a shield and sword.

"I don't understand how you fight anyone in this helmet," he said.

"That is not a battle helmet," she explained. "It is ceremonial. It is to . . . uh, puff out your chest. They would wear leather caps in battle."

Trin and I continued to snap away with our cameras. With his pant legs rolled up like Euro-style capris, Bojo looked kind of like a dorky American engineer who'd wanted to avoid getting the cuffs of his pants dirty and then ended up in a replica Viking hut wearing a helmet and bunch of animal pelts that didn't fit him. If you squinted, I mean.

When Bojo finally disrobed and handed back the replica Viking gear, I saw that we had come to the unfortunate denouement of the historical re-enacting relationship where we wanted to leave and continue on with our trip, and this woman wanted—well, it was unclear. A tip? For us to stay and ask more questions? She kept repeating, "What other questions do you have?" And the British couple or Trin would dutifully ask, "So, the spoons? They made them out of wood?"

"Now you give me four-thousand krónur," she said, basically out of the blue.

I forced a laugh, but it was totally unclear if she was joking because she said it while staring at the fire without blinking.

Trin looked to me, asking with his eyes if we should tip this woman the equivalent of $24, and I could see I was going to have to be the hero here, take matters into my own hands and *Dark Knight* our way the fuck out of this awkwardness.

"Welp!" I said, clapping my hands together and stepping right in front of the British couple so that they had to take several steps deeper into the mud hut and away from the entrance, thus throwing them under the bus. "Thanks so much, that was really interesting." And I scuttled my two friends out of the hut and into daylight where the crazy eyes of old Icelandic women could never reach us again.

[**Total hero. I might as well have carried those two outside in my arms or one slung over each shoulder.**]

Walking back to the car, I noted, "I'm convinced the people who do historical re-enactments are half-yearning for a time when everyone lived with syphilis and died before the age of 40."

"Are we sure that woman was being paid to do that by anyone?" said Bojo. "I'm leaning toward her just being some lady who shows up, sits in that hut, and talks about Vikings. Probably the Icelandic Historical Society comes by to do maintenance every few months and they're like, 'Hey, Johanna, you can't sleep here. And stop trying to dress up tourists in the animal pelts.'"

**Inside Joke #19:** Bojo and Trin kept repeating the line, "Why! Why?! Why?!!" apropos of nothing, the cadence of each "why" rising to Seinfeldian heights.

Before leaving for Iceland, Bojo and Trin had lived together with another one of our friends for about two years. During that period, they had the occasional party. During one such party when Bojo's two younger brothers were visiting, I got really drunk and passed out on a couch they'd moved into the kitchen to clear living room space for dancing/mingling. I mean, I got really fucking drunk. So drunk that during the night they placed a little Styrofoam cooler beside my head into which I vomited an impressive amount of former gut-belongings. There the cooler sat beside my head while I slept on the couch well into the afternoon while Trin, Bojo, his two brothers, and our other friend cleaned the entire apartment. By two in the afternoon, I was still passed out on the couch with my barf cooler next to me. Finally one of Bojo's brothers dripped a little dirty mop water down my back to wake me up, to which my response was to crumple into a ball and shout, "Why! Why!? Why?!!" Apparently everyone found this totally hilarious. But not me. I sprung to life, grabbed my jacket, and left with my box of puke under my arm, the contents sloshing as I went down the stairs.

It's kind of one of those things you had to be there for.

## Cabin on the Cliff

Trin had found a cabin in a small town called Skagastron (Skagaströnd, which we basically pronounced correctly!) on Airbnb.com, so rather than staying in another hostel where Bojo would knock up another French glacier researcher (his seed growing in her with *Species*-level rapidity) we got a place to ourselves for the night. The cabin had one tiny kitchen/living room space, a bedroom and a loft. Because Trin and Bojo are so go-along, get-along, when I dropped my bag in the bedroom to claim it, they didn't so much as challenge me to a game of Rock, Paper, Scissors or Pick-up Sticks to see who got it.

I was keen on this because of the whole masturbation situation. The situation being that I hadn't done it in like a week, which may be a lifetime record.

**[The previous record being 18 hours.]**

On the drive from Erik's Store I'd been complaining loudly about this.

"Yeah, it's a problem," said Bojo. "I don't even masturbate all that much. I do it to keep my prostate healthy. But even for me this is extreme."

"I'm quickly working toward a night emission here," I said. "I'm about ready to hump this coffee cup."

"Well, it will just be the three of us in this cabin tonight," Bojo said, and I looked at him, puzzled.

"So we can all jerk off in front of each other?" I asked. "Is that what you're saying?"

He shrugged. "I was not aware you were ever that shy about it."

Yet much to my dismay I was too exhausted to take care of business, and this bed—Jesus Christ, this bed in this cabin in Skagaströnd, Iceland—it was the most comfortable fucking thing I'd ever laid down on in my entire life.

*Fuck those sitting-up sleeping Vikings*, I thought when my head hit the pillow. *Fuck. Oh, fuck that's comfortable*, I continued as my head descended deeper into the pillow. There was some kind of padding between the mattress and the sheets, padding like a silk-stuffed cloud. *Goddamnit, no, Markley, no—touch yourself. Do it, man! This is your only chance. Just do it. Just get it done, please; you'll regret it if you miss this—Oh, God, what's the thread count on these sheets like 30,000? I can't even feel my skin anymore. Oh, God, what is that, an elf sprinkling glitter on my face and twirling a baton? Oh Christ, I'm dreaming, aren't I? I'm already asleep, aren't I?*

At any rate, before the elf came with his magic glitter, the three of us hiked up the rock embankment behind the cabin to the top of a cliff that looked out over the Húnaflói Sea, an inlet that leads to the Arctic. We watched the sun set at midnight, the yellow orb lowering just below the horizon and then sitting there, glowing with all the majesty your imagination can never come up with. In my delirium, I watched the yellow-pink light wane and thought about the owner of a restaurant we'd met that day in some town, the name of which I'll never remember, just another one of these blip-on-the-map coastal villages with one gas station, one grocery, and one pizza-and-burger joint claiming to have the best pizza and burgers in town. We were the only customers in the place, and we sat under a picture of a Scottish sailor smoking a pipe. The proprietor, a middle-aged man in an apron, made us each a meal like he was our dad—ham-and-cheese sandwich for me—and when we finished, he asked us about our trip, so we told him, and he asked us where we were from, and even though it wasn't exactly true in every sense, we always told people Chicago because they've heard of that, and he started talking about how he'd lived in America once, in Seattle, where he'd worked in a garage as a mechanic, and the garage was owned by the father of the girl he loved, but "things didn't work out," and the platitude "things didn't work out" seems to translate into every language, an easy way of glossing over the heartache of losing your best friend, but when it didn't work out between him and this girl whose father he worked for, he rented a car and drove down the Pacific Coast Highway, and he finished, way too sadly, "That was long ago, way back. That was when I was young and good looking." And with the sun gone but the sky still bright as day, I climb back down the rock face and into the most incredible bed on the planet and my story and my best friend and this man and his girl's father's garage and that elf all got mixed up in my dreams.

## Cream Cheese

Before viewing *Gnarr* on iTunes that night, Bojo and Trin had gone for a run, only to discover that the box that heated the shower's water wasn't working, so they both had to go to bed sticky and disgusting—the cabin being way too cold to brave a cold shower. In the morning, though, I was determined to get a hot shower and spent a few minutes investigating the situation. Finally, I found the breaker box, started guessing at what word meant "bathroom" in Icelandic, and flipped the breaker like I was choosing which wire to cut on a bomb. Disco—hot water galore!

"How fucking handy is this motherfucker?" I taunted Bojo, still half-sleeping on the couch and Trin, half-sleeping in the loft.

"I think my penis actually just grew. One of you check it to see how much it's grown. With your mouth!"

"Hmm, so you're out of the negative numbers," murmured Bojo.

"You're both engineers. You've got your fancy degrees in building shit and doing math and along comes this meek little humanities major who spent all of college reading poetry, and I jam it up both your asses with my handy brilliance."

My braggadocio proved premature because when we went to make breakfast we discovered we didn't have any butter with which to cook the 10 eggs we'd bought. During our trip we'd been eating nothing but eggs and *skyr* for breakfast. *Skyr* being the Icelandic style of yogurt, which is actually a "fresh acid-set cheese." *Skyr*, to be sure, is probably one of the most delicious cultured dairy products I've ever eaten. The three of us were housing the stuff by the bucketful each morning.

"We could hard-boil them," Trin suggested for the eggs.

"What about cream cheese?" I asked. "We still have a bunch of it left over from the lox."

"Can you cook with cream cheese?" he asked.

"Why not? It's a buttery-type thing."

"I think I'll hard-boil mine."

Feeling bold because I'd figured out the breaker box, I plowed ahead, slapped a big glop of cream cheese into a pan, and cooked my eggs. Which leads me to:

**Iceland Travel Tip #98:** You cannot cook anything in cream cheese. The cream cheese will just burn to the pan, forming a nasty brown skin that smells like burnt cheese. You will then go ahead and eat the eggs you tried to cook in it so as not to look like a moron in front of your friends, and these eggs with their burnt-cream-cheese flavoring will taste like day-old cannibal shit.

## The Zombie Apocalypse Redoubt

Normally a news-junkie, while traveling in Iceland I forced myself to read as little news from the States as possible because, you know, I was on vacation and didn't care to be depressed by the thought of an impending Mitt Romney presidency. Besides, travel should be about getting outside your regimen. I wasn't working out, I wasn't writing and reading every day, and I wasn't even watching the NBA playoffs. However, even in my experience-life mode, it was impossible to not hear about what was going on in America, specifically that the long-awaited zombie apocalypse seemed to have kicked off. You may remember this period of history, as successive news events appeared to make clear that it was time to arm ourselves with shotguns and chain saws and board up the farmhouse.

The craze began with the story of Rudy Eugene, who was shot and killed by police after he attacked a drifter on Miami's heavily trafficked MacArthur Causeway. A surveillance video showed Eugene walking naked along the causeway until he found the drifter and proceeded to attack him by *eating his fucking face*. Police arrived 15 minutes later, and an officer shot Eugene, at which point, according to an eyewitness, Eugene "looked up at the officer growling and with a strip of flesh in his mouth even after being struck by the first bullet." It took six shots to bring Eugene down, a truly zombie-like number of bullets. At first, authorities blamed the psychotic behavior on a synthetic drug associated with bath salts, but toxicology reports indicated the only drug in his system was marijuana. Eugene's victim survived, but lost 80% of his face, everything except a bit of beard and his right eye (meaning the left ended up in Eugene's stomach). No word on whether that drifter has now tried to eat someone himself.

A day later police were called to the house of Wayne Carter in Hackensack, N.J. For unknown reasons, Carter had barricaded himself inside of the house with a knife, and when police broke the door down, Carter went about stabbing himself repeatedly in the stomach and then throwing pieces of his flesh and intestines at the police. They tried to subdue Carter with pepper spray, but this only seemed to enrage him further, and it eventually took a whole SWAT team to bring Carter down and get him to a hospital.

Then in a Maryland suburb, a college student named Alex Kinyua was arrested for using a knife to carve up an older man. After ranting about human sacrifice on Facebook and displaying other bizarre behavior, he admitted what he'd done to a friend of his father's named Kujoe Bonsafo Agyei-Kodie. He also admitted that he'd eaten the man's heart and parts of his brain.

Finally, there's the story of Luka Rocco Magnotta, the bisexual porn actor and gay escort, who kidnapped a Chinese student from Concordia University in Montreal. He stabbed the guy to death with an ice pick, dismembered parts of the body, and mailed them to Canada's top political parties—but not before cannibalizing and sexually defiling the corpse, filming the whole thing, and posting it on the internet. The Conservative Party got a severed foot, the Liberal Party a severed hand, and on the video Magnotta is seen eating a piece of buttock flesh. Magnotta was finally caught in Berlin but not before freaking everyone out on his international flight by growing agitated and heading to the back of the plane to weep uncontrollably.

Media buzz of a zombie apocalypse even prompted the Centers for Disease Control to issue a for-real press release saying not to worry, there was no evidence of a zombie apocalypse under way, which, let's face it, is exactly what the government would say to keep people from panicking during the zombie apocalypse.

We left the cabin that morning, and the relatively flimsy walls and multiple low windows sparked much debate as to whether we could defend ourselves from zombies within its confines. The general consensus was no, but should it begin, I argued to Trin and Boj that Iceland would still be the perfect place to weather the storm of deranged flesh-eating maniacs.

"Think about it: We're on an island nation with a bunch of beautiful girls; it has its own renewable, geothermal power source, so we can always keep the lights on, and there are low temperatures in the winter so it's harder for zombies to survive—"

"Hold on," said Bojo. "Who said zombies can't survive the winter?"

"C'mon, man, these aren't bullshit fairy tale zombies that can walk on the sea floor or that can only be killed with a bullet to the head. This ain't some bullshit Rapture story where the dead walk the earth. This is science, man. These zombies will have to, you know, obey the laws of physics and physiology, which means they're just super-strong, strung-out crazy people trying to eat your fucking face. Science, dude! That means if we're in Iceland, and Iceland goes into quarantine, we can keep them out more effectively than the States with its impossible-to-defend borders. Worst comes to worst, we retreat to the center of the island where the terrain is so inhospitable that crazy zombie people won't be able to survive longer than a couple days. We build a compound and let beautiful girls hang out and maybe try to set up a hot spring pool of some kind."

"Wow, you've really thought this out," said Trin from the backseat.

"I'm a man of action, buddy. Now do you want in on my zombie apocalypse redoubt or not?"

"I want in on it even if there is no zombie apocalypse."

## Curse of the Vacation Pictures

"Let's walk down there," said Trin.

"What? No, c'mon, man. We need to keep moving."

"It'll take like five minutes."

"And we have like five hours of driving left today."

The largest source of tension in our three-person group dynamic came from Trin's insistence on spending an hour taking pictures at every single spot of geographically feasible soil and my need for perpetual motion, always running away from what I have, looking for the next best thing. Trin is a stop-and-smell-the-roses-until-you've-been-there-so-long-they-wilt-and-regrow kinda guy whereas I am a Chairman of the Joint Chiefs of Staff of travel. I've got ambitions. I want to work my way up the ranks to Supreme Allied Commander of Getting to the Next Fucking Hostel. This difference of personality manifested itself in our weapons of choice. For his seven-month sojourn, Trin purchased a really nice, expensive digital camera and tripod. He photographed basically everything we came across. There is a rock in Skagaströnd that is still blushing from the attention Trin gave it. I, on the other hand, find taking pictures kind of boring and feel about vacation pictures the same way I feel about looking at pics of friends' babies: I'll check out one or two and then I want you to leave me the fuck alone. You know when someone gets back from a trip and tries to foist upon you all 500 pictures of their experience? ("This is me reading a book on the train." "Here's a nice brioche I tried, though it was a little dry." "Here's a church, but I forget why it's supposed to be important? I guess it has some fresco painting by someone famous." "This is Alex, our sommelier in Madrid—he was the nicest; he gave us complimentary mints!").

This phenomenon was obnoxious enough when the only technology was Polaroid cameras, disposable cameras, or cameras with finite amounts of film that you had to pay to have developed. With the advent of the camera phone, it's downright unbearable. For me, pictures never look particularly special and certainly they never approach the power of the image felt in the moment of its first impression from orb to brain. Yet I took pictures as well, just pointing my Coolpix and snapping away without really looking, just sorta hoping that one of them will turn out to be interesting. Mostly, I spent my time jotting notes to myself, keeping a pen and pad of paper handy wherever we went. Sometimes it was Iceland-related and sometimes it was just the normal weird stuff that occurs to me as brilliant insight.

**[These include but are not limited to: "Shredded wheat is all well and good, but you always end up with that shredded wheat dust at**

the bottom of the cereal box." "Still need to read Dawkin's *The Selfish Gene*—you've literally been meaning to do that for 10 years now." "Butts that pop are better than religion."]

Some people like the image to bring them back to a time and place while some enjoy everything through the scrim of memory, for whom the two-dimensional interpretation feels staged and impersonal. Having said all that, on this trip I did get a pretty sweet picture of Bojo pretending to levitate a balloon with his index finger.

Two places we spent an inordinate amount of picture-taking time illustrate how I am both correct and incorrect in my photographalaise.

First, we drove 10 minutes out of our way to a little hamlet we called "Gumbear" (Glaumbær) to see an example of 18th- and 19th-century turf houses. Turf houses are actually works of relatively ingenious construction because—think about it—in those centuries we will call the "olden times," the Icelandic didn't have modern building materials or a whole lot of ways to keep themselves warm during brutal winters. They also had (and continue to have) an extreme dearth of large trees to an extent that most people in forested parts of the world cannot understand. Seriously, most of Iceland's "forests" are patches of short pines that look more like those Christmas tree lots that spring up after Thanksgiving. Turf houses use thin wooden shells with grass turf, which grows thick and in abundance, stuffed between the shells. The same turf then coats the roof, which is sloped at a very particular angle to keep it from leaking in the winter and drying out in the summer. Incredibly, these structures could last up to a century.

Of course, now the Icelandic have concrete, so the turf houses of Gumbear are a small tourist destination. We spent half an hour walking around the grassy knobs protruding from the earth, taking pictures, feeling the roof material, as organic as any hillside, and getting attacked by flies that appeared not to fear the harried swatting techniques of irritated American tourists. I strolled inside a replica of an old farming shed, knocked over a whole slew of old-timey farming equipment when I tried to pick up a shovel, and too late saw the sign that told me not to touch anything. Trin and I wandered into the main entrance to the turf houses where a skinny, awkward teenage girl explained that it would be 800 krónur to enter.

"Ah, Takk," said Trin. Then as we left, "Takk, but no Takk, lady."

"This reminds me so much of elementary school field trips in Ohio," I told him. "When they'd take the whole class to see an Amish barn, and we'd have to hear about antique plowing equipment for five hours, and we all kind of just stood around looking at each other like, 'When the fuck is this bullshit gonna be over? I'd rather be doing multiplication tables.'"

Therefore, at Gumbear, I could have taken a quick snapshot, read the little plaque about resilient Icelandic settlers, and found somewhere to pee—in and out in five minutes. The Oxna-sump-in-sumpin Pass (Öxnadalsheiði, derived from Trin saying, "OK, I think the next thing is the Oxna . . . uh, Oxna-somethin-some-thin.") is a different story.

The problem with driving around Iceland is that you're confronted by a new soul-enriching, breath-taking, life-affirming natural sight every five goddamn minutes. It's totally exhausting. This pass, however, really did bowl us all over. You come down the highway through the mountains and the road runs to the valley floor. By some awesome geological mojo, these plateaued, snow-capped mountains rise on either side of the pass while a small river crisscrosses beneath the road feeding bright green fields. At the end of the pass, the flat mountains suddenly give way to this collection of peaks called Pyerbrekkuhnjukur (we didn't even bother coming up with a fake name for that one) that spike violently into the sky. It's a dinosauric, *Dark Tower*-esque, evil empire-looking mountain range. On the valley floor we spent a long, long time with our cameras. Trin knelt by the river and captured the water running over the rocks, and I lay on my back and took pictures of the cotton-ball clouds in the blue sky overhead.

I have no idea how long we stayed there.

# FIVE

# The Road Trip Continues

"Myvan" (Mývatn) literally means "lake of the midges," and we'll get to those little bastards in a second, but it's more important to know that Mývatn exists in an area of extreme geologic activity, including the Krafla volcano (spelled exactly as it sounds; was that so hard, Icelandic language?). The whole northeast region of Iceland has basically been subjected to endless earthquakes and eruptions for most of the island's history. It is scarred with myriad formations of that activity. Mývatn is a eutrophic lake, which just means it has a ton of nutrients like phosphorous and nitrogen, so aquatic plants and algae grow like gangbusters.

Supposedly home to some of the best trout fishing in the world, the Laxa River provides drainage from Mývatn to the North Sea, and in 1970 it became the sight of one of the most dramatic political protests in Icelandic history. The government decided it wanted to dam the Laxa, and farmers in the valley behind the dam were none too pleased with this. After exhausting all of their legal options to no avail, they decided to plant dynamite at the construction site. By this I do not mean a conspiracy of four or five disgruntled Ted Kaczynski types. More than 200 farmers turned out on the fateful night, with some of them driving tractors to dig the hole and others delivering and setting off the dynamite. In a testament to hardheaded Icelandic gusto, while 65 farmers were convicted and merely fined, many more *attempted to get themselves prosecuted for the crime*. Even more unbelievably, Iceland's Supreme Court eventually overturned the fine.

"We ought to earn the Nobel Peace Prize," one of the dynamiters told a reporter, "since we actually used Nobel's invention to re-establish peace between man and nature."

Just south of Mývatn, we toured enormous craters where massive blobs of magma crashed into the earth the last time Krafla erupted. The craters stretch across farms; they're longer than basketball courts, and it was incredible to think of the lava raining down from the sky and exploding into the ground, the rings of black sand looking like fresh scorch marks. We milled about for a bit while the sheep and horses of a nearby farm gazed at us thoughtfully. In the distance, a beautiful snow-capped plateau called Blafjall looked like a white crown sitting atop the beige fields, stretching away, positively Delphian, to the south. It's difficult to describe the grandeur of all these sights, but there's something enormous about Iceland. Everything there seems to command your attention, seems to spread across the Earth in such a way that you think "this thing, this right here thing" is the world's crowning geologic achievement. Yet it's all so new and impermanent, the shifting seismic activity beneath our feet virtually guaranteeing that a day will come when it will be no more.

From there, we drove north to Dimburger (Dimmuborgir), a series of trails amidst lava fields punctuated by lava pillars. About 2,300 years ago lava from nearby volcanoes flowed over a small lake causing the water to boil. The rising steam created these craggy towers that really do look like "dark castles" as the name suggests. The three of us took the longest trail and wound our way through the black rock, chatting idly.

In Icelandic Christian mythology, Dimmuborgir is supposedly where Satan fell after God got fed up with him in heaven. A helpful sign also told us it was allegedly home to the Yule Lads, which are like the Icelandic version of Santa Claus. Instead of one jolly, bearded fat man, you get 13 brothers with names that, when translated into English, sound like *Snow White and the Seven Dwarfs* meets fetish pornography, including: "Pot-Scraper," "Sausage-Swiper," "Spoon-Licker," "Door-Slammer," "Bowl-Licker," "Yogurt-Gobbler," and "Stubby." My favorite Wikipedia description ever, of all time, period, has to be for the Yule Lad *Stekkjastaur*: "Harasses sheep, but is impaired by his stiff peg legs."

And really isn't that universal? I think there may be a little *Stekkjastaur* in all of us.

Along our hike through the solidified, fragmented lava, the three of us somehow got on the topic of women from our pasts.

I guess at some point when you hang out with friends for long enough, you always end up there. I won't go into too many of the gory details, but suffice it to say, the three of us all had this one part of our lives in common: that we'd been with someone and it hadn't worked out—that phrase even old men in Iceland know. But we were getting to that age when our friends had all begun to marry or at least settle down with a significant other. We were relieved to be here, to have the ability to pick up and go without explaining that we just weren't ready for the adventure to be over yet.

"I got to the point where I was like, OK, so I'm going down this road, but there are all these things I wanted to do, that I always told myself I would do," said Trin, speaking of a girl he dated for five years. "I was never single in my 20s, I never traveled as much as I wanted to, and it sucks because for women I think there is a good biological reason to be with someone when you're young. You know, I want to have a family someday. I get that."

"But it doesn't make as much sense if you're a guy," said Bojo. "You have a lot of time to figure that stuff out. That's what Trin's dad was basically telling us right before we left for New York. And I don't want to wait until I'm retired to get out and do things, which is the way I feel a lot of people end up doing it."

"I mean, biology aside, I think even if you're a woman, there's every reason to hold off as long as possible," I added. "I don't know. I just always think about how incredibly easy it is to get other places now. Like it's a recent advent, this idea that you can travel basically anywhere in the world, and I don't think we culturally appreciate that the way that we should. It's still hard, though, you know? Like this trip that we're doing as cheap as we can—it's still going to be fucking expensive. And to find the time off, the time away from your life and working—it's difficult. And for a lot of people with student debt or career paths that require non-stop work—"

"Like the way my job was," said Bojo.

"Exactly. I just always think about that. How the opportunity to connect and interact and get places you never thought you could has never been better in the history of human civilization. And sometimes I think part of what you give up when you want to ride that path is the ability to have that nuclear relationship with someone else."

"For now," said Trin.

"For now," I agreed, although I was unsure if I did.

# Hell

On our way to Krafla, we passed the village of Reykjahlíð and saw a church. This church stood in place of another church, where, in 1729 during the eruption of the Krafla volcano known as the Mývatn Fires, the lava flows wiped out the rest of the town but stopped just before overtaking the church, supposedly due to the prayers of the village priest inside. This led to me picturing an exhausted God, doling out answers to prayers all over 1729 Christendom, at the last second going, "OK, John, son of the blacksmith, you may have respite from your wretched cough, and Talia Le Piex, pious French schoolmarm, I grant you the child for your previously barren womb, and *Oh, dear Me! The church! That church in Iceland with all the lava flowing toward it! I command the lava to stop!*"

To get to Krafla, you wind over a mountain and into a crater with land that looks like the surface of Mars. The road passes one of Iceland's many geothermal energy plants, steam rising from this building that looks like a package of metal yogurt containers. The Krafla power station produces about 60 megawatts of energy since it reached full production capacity in 1999. Geothermal energy, which to put it as simply as possible, basically means using the pools of magma beneath the island to heat water that creates steam and turns turbines thereby producing electricity, provides 26 percent of Iceland's energy and 83 percent of its heating requirements (like for hot water and to heat some city streets from below during the winter). With the other 73.8 percent of its energy needs coming from hydro-power, only 0.1 percent of Iceland's power comes from fossil fuels, and the government has the goal of powering itself entirely by renewables in the near future. With electric cars in their infancy of replacing the internal combustion engine, this is not unrealistic.

After we passed the Krafla station, we arrived at the crater Viti, which means Hell. Hiking around the rim of the crater, we got some of the trip's most colorful pictures—Viti's bright blue pool of melted snow and ice with geothermal steam rising and snow-capped mountains as far as the eye could see.

"It's unclear to me if this is a path or we're just walking through bad parts of a volcano," I said, loose rock and sand skittering out from under my foot.

"No, there's a string," said Trin, pointing to the small cord, which seemed to delineate a path.

"And a sign that says, 'Warning: This area is dangerous, you idiot. Go back,'" said Boj.

The "trail" took us down to a small valley of the crater where more of an effort had been made to keep moron tourists from leaving the safe areas. Having worked in Grand Teton National Park, which is just south of Yellowstone with its raging geothermal activity, I was well aware of what super-heated pools of water can do to a person. Every year at Yellowstone some jackass seems intent on getting horrendous burns, usually by trying to take a picture in an unsafe area or something equally mundane. I knelt to take a picture of a small cerulean pool, bubbling mud and clay. Through the knee of my jeans I could feel the warmth, hot and ancient and clawing at the earth holding it back. You could picture the Devil scratching at the ceiling of his kingdom.

On the way back, we stopped at one of the sites we'd sworn to hit. No, not the Krafla geothermal pool, which we deemed too expensive if we were also going to make a trip to the Blue Lagoon geothermal spa in Reykjavík, but a toilet sitting out in the middle of a gravel lot beside a working shower fixture.

Believe me, I spent a good day Googling "Krafla toilet," "Krafla commode," and other variations, and while others had certainly witnessed and photographically documented the Krafla outdoor toilet, no one appeared to have an explanation for what its purpose might be. We, however, found a purpose, and spent the next 20 minutes giggling and pretending to take pictures of ourselves pooping. Believe me, were it an old-fashioned camera instead of a digital, I would have used up at least one roll of film trying to capture Trin squatting over the bowl while attempting to not let the seat of his jeans actually touch the porcelain.

Ah, travel, love, life . . .

## Icelandic Wildlife

Iceland has unique and wonderful wildlife and domesticated animal species. Here are some high- and low-lights:

**Midges:** Fuck midges. No, seriously: we are in the sixth great extinction event in the history of planet Earth, and as long as we take those little fuckers with us, I'm not going to complain anymore. A midge is a little fly-like insect that doesn't bite but flies around your face and into your mouth and ears and eyes like it's the Millennium Falcon in the maw of one of those space parasites. As we discovered, they are not confined to the Lake of the Midges. At one point, a midge flew into my ear, and days later I swear I could still feel it scatting around in my eardrum. Eventually, we heard this tip that seemed to work: Midges are apparently attracted to the highest point of the creature they're annoying, which on humans is obviously your head. If you raise your fist to the sky, they'll congregate around that instead. Of course, this also meant that Trin, Bojo, and I would be hiking along looking like we were trying to start a Black Power movement.

**Roadrunner-Looking Bird:** There was this bird that looked very much like the Roadrunner of the famous cartoons, but it could fly. We kept noticing this roadrunner-looking bird because the species apparently did not know about the agreement made famous by the *Seinfeld* episode where George hits a pigeon that doesn't get out of the way of his car. The agreement between birds and humans in vehicles is that when we drive at them, they move. This bird, however, kept failing to heed our speeding Hyundai i20, and Bojo could never reconcile whether he really wanted to brake for this annoying asshole bird. We never hit one, but all of us agreed if we did, it would only be because they had it coming.

**Sheep:** The minister in Halldór Laxness's *Independent People* "never wearied of denouncing sheep and slandering that animal species, for it was his opinion that they seduced the hearts of men from God." Icelandic sheep occasionally made us wonder who was wearing the pants in the man-sheep relationship. Basically, anywhere outside of Reykjavík sheep think they own the place. They meander in the roads, baa at you constantly, and when you try to take pictures of them on the other side of a fence, as we did when we stopped at the southern end of Mývatn, the babies come up to you baaing in a way that seems like they're saying, "Hey! You! Stand there! Look funny! Be my amusement! Put your hand out! I wanna lick it! I wanna lick it! I wanna lick it!" Then the mother follows her young ones protectively, also baaing at you, but seeming to say, "Hey, douche bag! Get outta here, douche bag! You like sheep kids, you sick douche bag? Go back to farming, you useless douche bag!" Here are my three favorite Icelandic sheep sights:

- On the second day of the trip when we hadn't come to fully understand just how many sheep we would be seeing, we stopped at a bridge to take some pictures of the lake it ran across. Trin spotted a mother sheep and a few baby sheep eating some grass, as sheep are wont to do, and decided to take a few pictures. The baby sheep both looked up at him, followed by the mother. They stopped eating grass and stared while Trin snapped away. Then the mother sheep kinda sorta fake-charged Trin, basically just making a head feint—kind of like a jab step in basketball—and Trin went sprawling backward, athletically, mind you, but still getting ready to run for his life from this mommy sheep.

- Often you would see baby sheep milking from their mothers. Therefore it appeared from my juvenile perspective that the sheep were blowing each other, but this one time we drove by what were clearly two adult sheep doing nasty stuff. Specifically, one of the sheep was pretty clearly eating the other one's ass. It was impossible for me to tell if this was a sex thing or maybe a hygienic-type favor, but I saw what I saw, which was one sheep giving another sheep the best-looking rim-job I'd seen in ages. When I pointed this out to the guys, Bojo said, "Steve, you really do need to masturbate tonight. Just find a way."

- While crossing through the Oxna-sumpin-sumpin valley we were driving beside the river with the sun to the right of the car. From the passenger seat, I spotted a small rise in the earth beside the river so that this golden plain came to a kind of ridge, and on this perch stood three sheep stoically watching the river. The largest, a male with harsh, curving horns, was flanked by two smaller ones, maybe his sons. The sunlight hit them in such a way that they appeared to stand in a spotlight of silken gold, the brown grass glowing all around them. It was like *The Lion King* but in real life. And with sheep. I could almost hear the Sheep King saying to his sons, "One day, this magnificent kingdom will be yours."

**Reindeer:** I never saw a reindeer, but Trin did. This was because I'd taken over driving, and the roads of southern Iceland have numerous warnings to watch for reindeer crossing. Apparently, he caught sight of them to the car's right, but I dared not crane my head back. As a result I have no reindeer story to put here, and my life is a failure.

**Horses:** Icelandic horses, or "horsies" in the preferred nomenclature of me pointing from the front seat and calling it out excitedly, happen to be a unique, specific species of horse that developed only in Iceland, which has very specific laws to maintain the rarity of the species. It's illegal to import horses and once a horse has left Iceland it can never return.

**[Wait—how is that not a Disney movie yet? A baby horse gets separated from its parents and finds itself unable to return home and through a series of misadventures, pluck, and perhaps a quirky, quick-talking badger sidekick voiced by Seth Rogen, somehow journeys back to the pastures of its youth? Meeting along the way a sexy-eyed she-horse that all the dads taking their kids to the movie sort of find attractive? I just wrote that screenplay in like 30 seconds. Hey, Pixar, get at me!]**

Scandinavian settlers shoulder most of the credit for breeding the species. However, brutal winters and starvation also culled the herd, not to mention a 1780 volcanic eruption almost wiped out the species entirely. The breed is smaller than most horses, almost pony-sized. Most notably, the horses all have unique, totally hilarious haircuts. I mean, I'm not one who tends to find animals particularly amusing (I have no patience for YouTube videos of kittens and were I president I would try to ram a bill through Congress to outlaw them), but these horses were just so funny. They have these weird flowing manes that look like hairstyles on glam rock stars and B-movie actors. I swear I saw horse incarnations of Treat Williams and Don Johnson, not to mention David Bowie and Fabio (obvi). Some of the horses had a Flock of Seagulls cut (ask your parents) while others had Gold's Gym-style frosted tips. Most impressively, I saw a horse that was the spitting image of Gary Busey. Like if Gary Busey were transmorphed into a horse (via Disney cartoon?) that would have been this horse I saw.

**Ducks:** So there are ducks in Iceland, which is no biggie in and of itself, but I'm afraid I have to relate what we came to call the "duck incident." Be forewarned, this story does not make me at all proud: After we returned to Reykjavík, we used our last day with the i20 to hit up some sights along the Golden Circle, including Thingerville (Þingvellir), where the North American and Eurasian plates intersect. We left the car in the parking lot and went looking for the divide, and the path took us down by a thin inlet where a few families of ducks were kind of hanging out doing duck things. The first time we passed by without incident, and the two parent ducks, seeing us coming, led their baby ducks from the path out into the water.

"Hey, why don't you shut up, you stupid duck," Bojo said as we passed by.

Then on the way back, these ducks were again in our way, and again, the parents led the baby ducks back in the water. However, as we passed them, one of the two parent ducks, probably the mom, just whipped around and charged at us, snaking its head back and forth, hissing horribly. I'm totally embarrassed to say that we three full-grown men in peak physical condition all basically ran away. We stumbled backward, falling over each other to escape this terrifying duck. Having scared us off, the duck turned back and rejoined her flock, but our shame could not be so easily ignored.

"Did we all just run from that duck?" Trin asked.

"We can never tell anyone," said Bojo.

"Great," I said. "Now that duck is going to tell all its duck friends what a bunch of silly pussies we are."

I pictured that duck saying: "How is that the dominant species of the planet? I just charged and hissed, one little duck about a tenth of their size, one duck versus three of them, and they about shit their pants."

And that duck would be right, but then again, when it hissed, I saw into its duck mouth and down the concavity of its pink, grimy duck throat, and I can tell you if there is a place of terror and cruelty and horror outside of the temporal universe it would look like that.

## Akureyri

Akureyri (which, after a while, we actually began to pronounce semi-correctly "Ahk-oo-reh-ree") is Iceland's second largest town as long as you count all the surrounding suburbs of Reykjavík as one cityish entity. It's therefore known as the "capital of northern Iceland," but don't think that means it's this huge cosmopolitan place. As of the last census, it had just over 17,300 people, which is only a little larger than the small town I'm from in Ohio.

We got in to Akureyri after a long day of hiking around volcanic rims, and it was going to be our first night out in Iceland on a weekend when the bars were all open until 5 a.m. We were determined to make the most of it. This began with a beer and a cheap meal, which brings me to:

**Iceland Travel Tip #37:** If you're in Akureyri, make sure you go eat at a Parisian cafe called Bláa Kannan. For real. The address is Hafnarstræti 96. Go there. Not only did we have some of the cheapest, most delicious meals of the trip at this place, not only was it gorgeous inside with wood paneling, dark tables, and interesting art, but it had the most ridiculously cute college girls working there, all wearing the trademark tight black pants of the uniform. We became friendly with one girl, who became our unofficial advice-giver on Akureyri. Admittedly she was the first pretty girl we'd seen since we'd been on the road, but as I would discover this night, Bojo, Trin, and I were like flirting assassins. First of all, we had Trin with his five-day stubble, which was like looking into the sun. Then we had Bojo with his dark beard and cute little shy-goofy laugh. And then finally, we had me, a creature predisposed to saying stupid things to girls.

**[It is conventionally thought that you should say cool things to girls. This is incorrect. Being cool is so fantastically overrated because the only kind of girls you attract by being cool are girls who themselves think they are really cool. And the first law of coolness is that anyone who actually thinks they are cool—like actively believes it and therefore has no reservoir of insecurity—totally fucking sucks. Ergo, always say stupid things to girls that are generally indicative of your personality, like, "What's this bread made out of?" or "How do you say, 'What's this bread made out of?' in Icelandic?" or "*Jurassic Park* could totally happen."]**

Anyway, the barista-servers at Bláa Kannan just loved us and we got no shortage of smiles, errant eye contact, and totally unnecessary cleaning of tables near us. It should also be noted that the primary girl we became friendly with had probably the most awesome butt I've ever seen in my entire life. It was basically a perfect circle, the kind of derriere where it would not matter if your wife, mother, and ghost of your grandmother are sitting right by you—you have no choice but to look at it in awe, the reptilian part of your brain just kicking the normal pilot out of his chair and taking control. I took one of the cards with 30 stamp boxes for a free coffee. I only have one so far, but I am holding on to it.

We had only one night in Akureyri, but going out for a night in Iceland has a heady, epic feel. Every Friday is *The Iliad* and every Saturday is *The Odyssey*. We just kept meeting people, and the whole night was like one ass-long run-on sentence:

I was enjoying a beer in the lounge of the Backpacker's Hostel talking to some drunken Icelandic guy about NBA basketball because apparently the Icelandic love NBA basketball, and then we're approached by a kid from Oregon who's hitchhiking around the country, and he wants to tag along with us tonight, and he has a bottle of whiskey, which we all take pulls from when we get outside, just standing around in the street at midnight in what looks like early evening, and he's one of these guys with thick hipster glasses who looks like he walked off the stage from an Austin music festival, and this is all interesting but we gotta get to this bar, and inside immediately things get very fractured and strange because I spot two girls sitting by themselves, and I recognize them from the KEX hostel in Reykjavík, so I go over to say hello, and it turns out they are French-Canadian from Montreal, so I pull up a seat and we're talking—one short and cute with points to her teeth, the other tall and slim with a shock of curly blond hair and dark roots—and I mention to this girl that I've been following the student protests in Montreal, the city's college kids marching and occupying and causing great civil unrest over what they view as drastic increases in tuition, and this girl is pretty much blown the fuck away that an American knows about this, and she excitedly shows me the square of red cloth pinned to her jacket that signifies solidarity with the movement, which nearly every young person in Montreal has pinned somewhere, and just as I'm getting to know Myriam-Sofie and Charlotte, an old guy has approached Charlotte, petting her hair and whispering into her ear in that embarrassing, awkward, inappropriate way old guys have, and I'm looking around realizing I have no clue where Bojo and Trin have gotten to, and then I find Trin at the bar talking to a dude, and this dude is, like, *talking* to Trin, in that he has his arm slung around his shoulder and he's laughing and patting his back like they've been buddies for 50 years, and suddenly some other guy just walks right up to me and goes, "You guys are awesome!" and then walks away, and it's unclear to me what spurred that, but now this guy talking to Trin is taking off his shirt, and I head off to find Bojo, who is outside on the patio, talking to a bunch of old guys, one of whom looks exactly like Voldemort, with an evil bald head, and one of the other guys has bought Bojo an absurd number of shots, and Bojo tells me, "These guys are awesome," and then I'm benefitting from the friendliness of the Icelandic, and Trin comes hurtling up to us holding a black long-sleeved shirt—the shirt that guy was wearing, saying, "These people are great. That guy literally just gave me the shirt off his back," even though it's unclear why, but the mystery must be forever abandoned because I'm wrapped up in a conversation with one of these old guys, who follow the axiomatic rule that they love to tell young guys how to get laid, a situation that's true the world over, but especially in Iceland where they will only tell you how aggressive you must be, and suddenly Voldemort was saying to me, "I have the best pickup line for you—works every time," and I say, "OK, what's that?" and he goes, "You must go up to a girl, and say, 'Excuse me, I think my dick has died—can I bury it in your ass?' That line works every time," and I'm laughing, and so is Voldemort but in a way that appears he's not joking, but then these guys have a couple of older lady friends, and one of them has been eyeing Bojo like a piece of lamb, a little baby lamb she wants to eat, and her story is that she's a widow with four kids from a fishing village an hour away ("Hey, she had me at four kids," Bojo will later explain), and she keeps mentioning how close it is and how long it's been since she's had sex, and for me, there was really no way to tackle either of these subjects without feeling extremely uncomfortable, and then all those guys are taking us to a bar called the Post Office where the post office used to be, and it's all green lasers and fog machines, and at this bar, Trin meets a young blond girl (naturally) who he's dancing with while Bojo and I chat up her friends, and the blond girl is named Inga and her friend is named Eygló, and they have a third friend whose name just categorically will not stay in my brain no matter how many times she sounds out the syllables, and she's extremely pretty, and I am hitting on her with all the forwardness my feminist mother and respectful

Midwestern upbringing will allow because, like I told Voldemort, if you're from a middle-class family in the Midwest, you were likely "raised right," by which I mean, you don't say disgusting things to women in bars, and so I'm really drunk and torn between being like, "Hey, I'm Steve, a writer from Chicago, and I really like Iceland—it's such a beautiful country!" and "Hey, will you choke me with your bra while I spit in your mouth?" but before I could arrive at a decision, the Post Office is closing because it's 5 in the fucking morning with daylight still blazing, and as we all spill out into the street, these girls inform us that the night is not over because we have to go get pizza at this late-night place, and while we all wait crammed into this small pizza shop some D-bagish Icelandic guy is trying to hit on this love of mine, talking to her in Icelandic, which puts me at a very distinct disadvantage, but I'm guessing he's saying something along the lines of, "This American's boner is very small," but before long we're back out on the square in the center of the city where everyone is gathered in groups like the parking lot after a high school dance, and we're all sitting on the square eating pizza, and Inga explains that they can't invite us back anywhere because they are all staying with her grandmother, and wow does this put a crimp in our night's plans, and we're all brainstorming ways around this ("Can we put your grandmother in a shed of some kind for a while?"), and then the girls are telling us that they are throwing a party for National Day the next week, and this gal I'm hitting on will be singing at it, and they suggest we come, and I say something like, "Well, I'm only coming if we're making out," and she says, "No, you will come, and you must watch my 17-year-old sister and make sure she doesn't drink too much," and then she launches into this long plan she's apparently formed on the spot in which I will chaperone her 17-year-old sister during this raging, alcohol-soaked party, and Bojo is sitting beside me laughing his ass off at this—"Yeah," he would say later, "Steve Markley's exactly the guy I want looking after my hot, drunk, 17-year-old sister," and he cracks up all over again at this fox-in-the-henhouse scenario, and then the girls are all going home, but they want to hang out if we ever get back to Reykjavík, and there's some exchanging of emails, and finally Bojo, Trin, and I are heading back to the hostel, but it's pure daylight out now, the Arctic light attacking whatever part of the brain cocaine and methamphetamines work over because even though we spent the day hiking and even though we should be exhausted, sleep feels like the most distant notion right now, an idea for some other, lesser god, and we laugh and gallop down the street and dance like fools.

## The Hostel Situation

Look, don't get me wrong: I really recommend that everyone who travels take advantage of hostels. Hostels are great. They're cheap, and everyone who stays in them is a fellow traveler unafraid to have a conversation. Hotels are not only more expensive, but even the cheapest fosters a sense of exclusivity and reclusion. There is no common area; there is no sense of community. People keep to themselves. Hostels are where you go to hear stories. I've never stayed in a hotel when traveling outside of the U.S. Hostels get a big recommendation in that sense.

On the other hand, hostels also suck. You get the one anorexic pillow, and the one sheet you pull off the mattress because it makes no sense to pay another 10 bucks for the privilege of a bedspread. You stay in six-, eight-, and 10-person dorms where people are constantly getting up, moving around, snoring, coughing, thrashing in the bunk above you, trying not to fart. As if the never-ending daylight wasn't enough, I basically couldn't sleep in Icelandic hostels. I'd go into a light fog for a few hours but inevitably come to when the various sounds of all those bodies turned into an orchestra.

**[This included Bojo's nightly snoring, which was like the sound the hull of the Titanic likely made when it hit the iceberg, only phlegmier.]**

As Trin pointed out, every hostel we stayed in seemed to be under some kind of construction. Jack-hammering, nail guns, gasoline generators, hydraulic machines that seemed to do nothing but make noise. I woke up to all of these in Iceland, fuzzily asking no one, "What the fuck is that? Are they drilling geothermal wells outside?" Trin suggested that hostels paid for these projects just to get everyone out of bed and checked out on time.

## The Situation With Bojo's Driving

Bojo was and is a fine driver; don't get me wrong. Still, there's this one little thing that if I don't mention, my head might explode. Sitting beside him all those days in the car, I noticed he drank a lot of water, which is fine. However, this water was not fed via Camelbak into his cute little face, but by way of water bottle. He'd keep this bottle in between the seats and when he went to drink from it, he would hold the bottle in one hand, take his other hand off the wheel completely, and attempt to unscrew it. No knee on the wheel. The hand would leave and the car would inevitably begin to drift, so often the hand would shoot back to the steering wheel to correct. If we were on a straightaway with no cars around, he could complete the task, but if there was any curvature to the road whatsoever, his hand would shoot back and forth between steering wheel and bottle cap, unscrewing it in piecemeal actions like the Allied powers trying to cross the Rhine during World War I—a seemingly endless, pointless, fruitless, useless exercise in trench warfare, both sides dug in with no advantage (in this analogy, bottle cap versus hand).

I would sit there, tapping my foot, eyes darting back and forth between road and Bojo, nerves all but unraveling.

Hand to the cap, hand back to the wheel.

Hand to the cap, slight twist, no loosen-age, hand back to the wheel.

Hand to the cap, slight twist, some loosen-age, hand back to the wheel.

Hand to the cap, slight twist, moderate loosen-age, hand back to the wheel.

Hand to the cap, slight twist, total loosen-age but cap remains in place balanced precariously on lip of bottle, hand back to the wh—

*"What the fuck is the matter with you?"* I finally screamed. *"Have you never opened a bottle in a fucking car before? You're a goddamn engineer! You engineer shit! Stick a knee on the wheel to keep it steady while you perform this function that should take less than three seconds for a normal, able-bodied man. Or better yet— here's a wild fucking idea, Bojo!—clamp that goddamn water bottle*

*between your thighs, keep your hand on the instrument that controls the fate of all of our lives and use the pressure of your thighs to hold the bottle in place while you unscrew the cap with YOUR FREE HAND LIKE ANYONE ELSE WHO'S EVER UNSCREWED A CAP ON A BEVERAGE WHILE DRIVING SINCE MOTHERFUCKING TIME IMMEMORIAL!"*

OK, that's not a direct quote. It was more something like, "Hey, you need a hand with that?"

"Nah, I got it," he said. And we kept on driving.

## Friendship Equations

The next day took us by more pristine coastline, more snow-capped mountains, more lava fields covered in spongy green lichen, more gravel roads. Our big stop of the day was Dettifoss, Europe's most powerful waterfall. Scrambling over a field of gray geometric blocks of rock, we crossed this field that looks like an abandoned game of Tetris. Dettifoss comes tearing over a cliff with the fury of thunder, pounding the river below and sending up a mist that gathers in pinprick beads on your coat, skin, hair, and camera.

A rainbow arched perfectly over the falls. It's the kind of rainbow where you can, no shit, see every color as well as the point where it terminates in the rocks, walk up to it, and see no pot of gold. I took a lot of pictures of this.

"Steve Markley stops and smells the rainbows," said Bojo. The waterfall roared. You could watch the foamy waves hit the apex and kind of roll up and over the cliff's edge in slow-motion, nearly make out the individual gallons throwing up their hands to enjoy the roller coaster as they crested over the edge.

Earlier we'd hiked down from the road to the edge of a cliff overlooking the Jökulsá á Fjöllum, a river that sliced the earth into a magnificent valley with cliff faces rising on either side. On the hike back up, we started playing "Would You Rather."

Would You Rather is the most straightforward and entertaining of hypothetical games. Tapping into heterosexual males' innate fears of their own very obvious homosexual potential is one of the game's best angles.

"So, guys," I said, sweating through my jacket as we trudged back up the trail through the scrub brush. "Would you rather have the hottest girl you've ever seen—any girl of your choice—strap on a dildo and fuck you in the ass—"

"Oh God," said Bojo. "Steve, c'mon."

"—Or lie down on the ground while 10 guys jerk off on you?" I finished thoughtfully (usually I wait until the last possible second to design Option 2).

"Neither!" said Bojo, "I'll take neither."

"No. You can't pick neither. That's the point of the game. It's two unpleasant scenarios pitted against each other, and you must choose one. Bojo, you always make me explain the rules to you every time we play."

"I never want to play! You just start playing before anyone's agreed to play."

"Clearly the hot-girl-dildo-in-the-ass thing," said Trin.

"What? No way!" I said.

"I don't want 10 guys to come on me," said Trin.

"Not on the face. Just like on your chest. You can even wear goggles."

"Unnnh," said Bojo.

"You're saying you'd take the 10 guys jerking off on you?" Trin asked.

"Of course! That washes away. The dildo thing would just be uncomfortable. It's in your ass. I don't even like taking particularly big poops."

At this point, we were all kind of cracking up.

"Plus," I went on. "I masturbate in the supine position, so I'm used to having come on my chest."

Bojo was just shaking his head, his laugh stuttering out, his beard pulled thin by how far his smile had stretched. Believe it or not, this conversation actually got way more disgusting and way more bizarre to the point where even I—a guy who cares almost nothing about telling readers his preferred jerk-off positioning— refuse to write the rest down for historical documentation.

For whatever reason, though, this got the three of us talking about how we all knew each other and had come to have this conversation on a lonely hiking trail in northeastern Iceland about how much semen on one's chest is too much semen. To explain it, I'll need to make a complicated mathematical formula, and you'll need to remember the names Brian, Alex, and James.

Trin and Alex are friends from high school in Cleveland; Bojo lived across the hall from Alex during his freshman year at Miami University while Trin went to Georgia Tech. If x denotes long-standing friendships and + means a new friendship, we have:

**(Trin x Alex) + Bojo**

Alex then joined a fraternity at Miami where he met Brian; this is how Brian and Bojo also became friends, so:

**(Trin x Alex) + Bojo + Brian**

Meanwhile, Brian and James had lived together freshman year and after sophomore year moved into an apartment together. We will count that as a long-standing friendship, ergo:

**(James x Brian) + Bojo + (Alex x Trin)**

Finally, James and I roomed together when we studied in Italy one summer and became fast friends. The next summer we worked in Wyoming together, and the summer after that we moved to Chicago and became roommates. We'll count this as a long-standing friendship as well. At this point all the other friendships were long-standing. So:

**(Markley x James) x Brian x Bojo x Alex x Trin**

Finally, Brian, Bojo, Alex and Trin all ended up moving to Chicago, at which point we began hanging out together semi-regularly. Then James, my best friend in the city, left to go back to school, and I began hanging out with Bojo, Brian, Alex, and Trin. Thus:

**Markley + (Brian x Bojo x Alex x Trin)**

And by the time we were ready to go to Iceland, all those plus signs had become multiplication signs.

**[Is anyone following this? Can you tell I'm pathetic at math? Hell, I'm not even sure what's going on with these formulas, but I do know that when I came up with the idea while I was high, it sounded profound**

**in my head. Incidentally, that's also what happened to Joyce with *Ulysses*.]**

This is actually one of the unspoken pleasures of emerging adulthood that no one explains to you when you're younger: All the posing you did as a high school or college kid becomes unnecessary. You meet good, funny people, and that's it—you can just be friends. Think of the people you meet over the course of your life, and think of the ones who've stayed beside you even if you've moved great distances from each other, the ones who you could call up at a moment's notice if you had a flight diverted to their city and say, "Hey, can I crash with you? Oh, and would you want to stay up way too late drinking beer and catching up even though you have work tomorrow?"

It never fails to reassure me—about life in general, I guess—that the number of these people only seems to grow greater as you get older. Technically Bojo, Trin, and I were third-tier friends. Friends of friends' friends. Yet now we had this trip and more specifically this one moment of revolting conversation while plugging up a trail, and that moment is like a seed, right? There are so many moments that become the seeds we plant with each other, growing roots evermore.

Also, I just said "the seeds we plant with each other" which somehow, someway would make a great game of Would You Rather.

## The Seeker

It wasn't Bojo's persnickety habit with drinking water that made me want to take over behind the wheel, though. I just like driving.

After college I spent a year driving around the country, mostly out West with no one to take over. Like so many gas-guzzling Americans, I like the feel of a car, and I almost never get to drive now that I live in Chicago and take public transportation like a tree-hugging pussy. Almost immediately after I got behind the wheel, Trin and Bojo fell asleep on what happened to be a stretch of Highway 1 that couldn't have reminded me more of that trip across the Badlands all those years ago. From Dettifoss to the east coast there was nothing in this quadrant of Iceland in a way that you can't describe until you see so much nothing. Not a town, not a gas station, and barely even any other cars. After turning on to the main highway, I glanced at the clock on the dashboard, and when another car finally passed us going in the other direction, I realized it was the first car I'd seen in two hours.

Later I'd learn that this stretch of highway had only been paved about five years earlier, and the thought of going that distance over Iceland's sputtering gravel surfaces exhausted me just imagining it.

We were bound for the town of Seyosforor (Seyðisfjörður, though not incredibly difficult to pronounce—"Say-is-f-your-ur"—never stopped earning us corrections from the Icelandic), because the hostel there had been cheaper than the closer town of Eggs-at-the-store (Egilsstaðir). At the time, we did not realize that this town was not a mere fingernail away as indicated on the map, but rather we had to basically drive up and over a mountain. Now I've driven in a lot of different places in a lot of different situations (snow, downpours, mountain paths), but for a paved road in mostly clear weather, this drive was kind of butthole-puckering.

The switchbacks climbed the mountain's side. Our ears all popped. I crept around the hairpin turns and accelerated only slightly faster on the straightaways. Maybe two of the turns had guardrails, while the rest were just uncertain plummets down grassy cliffs.

"What the hell do they do in the winter?" I asked. "This is the only road into town. How does a truck with food do this?"

As we speculated, the road finally leveled out and we drove straight into the clouds, which hovered on the mountain's peak in thick globules that intermittently swallowed the car and stole our vision. Up here, there was snow everywhere. The road ran over a lake with massive chunks of ice floating in stillness. We got out at the first opportunity. The air was frigid, and the world up here seemed impossibly silent. The water, the ice, the clouds—none of them made sound. There was only the engine of the i20 idling and our voices ringing out across the mountaintop, echoing back at us as ghosts.

Needless to say, when we got back into the car, I was fascinated to see what the hell could possibly lay over the rise and below the clouds—what had possessed people to settle on the other side of this behemoth and build a road all the way up, over, and down. It didn't disappoint.

Seyðisfjörður looked like what would happen if *Twin Peaks* was nestled into a sweeping scene from *The Lord of the Rings*. The road winds gently down into this valley that is not majestic. "Majestic" is a word for whales or distant mountains—this was overwhelming. It overtook the eye. The town rested in a small harbor at the bottom of the valley while two massive mountain faces rose on either side, all slate-gray rock and verdant foliage, with waterfalls running like capillaries down their sides. The grass on the valley floor and rising up on the mountain faces was that color of a golf course, the kind you don't think exists in nature, and everywhere there was this ethereal mist that hung in different configurations as we descended.

We found our hostel in this miniscule town where the only bar had burned down, the one grocery was closed and the local girls seemed to circle the town in one car honking at the three of us. We got our own room in the hostel and took some time to set up our various computing devices. I wrote my column, and Trin updated his blog. In the meantime, Bojo found one of those books where visitors write little notes or draw pictures or just sign their names. He read it for a while, and then said, "Huh."

"What?"

"This entry."

Written in Spanish with a totally illegible signature, it was called "The Seeker." Bojo had taken several Spanish classes since college just for the heck of it, and though fluency remained out of his grasp, he could read it fairly well. He told me the writer began by talking about landing in Reykjavík. He was here because he was "looking for something missing in his life." The truth was he was having suicidal thoughts, many of them. And when he didn't find whatever it was he thought he might be looking for in Reykjavík, those thoughts grew deeper, darker. Driving across the country he randomly decided to come to this town. Maybe it was because on the map it looks like the end of the Earth. When he came over the same mountain pass that we did, he saw the valley with the town nestled in the harbor. The sun was breaking through the clouds and throwing light over the land. He wrote that this was the first moment he'd felt OK in a long, long time.

Now I don't know anything about this guy. He could have gone and hung himself a week later, but hearing what he wrote, I knew exactly what he was talking about. Not about suicidal thoughts, but about how you can get cornered in your own life. How all your dreams and aspirations, everything you thought about yourself and your journey can turn out wrong or deeply flawed, and you're only left wondering what exactly this leaves you with. When I tell people that this place, Seyðisfjörður, was my favorite of the trip and probably one of my favorite places I've ever been, that's why. Because we would see so many more things—another mountain pass on the way to Höfn that descended to a breath-catching ocean inlet and an azul pool of glacial water called Jökulsárlón and black sand beaches and huge fields of purple Alaskan lupine and craggy lava fields that stretched on to magnificent distances and Þingvellir where the tectonic plates meet and the Great Geysir of the southwest erupting skyward and a highway that curved around the coast with epic cliffs rising all around and waterfalls out of postcards and trails that ran through cleaved rock and the country's one forest of towering pines struggling to hold on in the soil—but when we came down the pass, and I saw this one obscure town, cradled in this one obscure place, and I literally couldn't take it all in, my eyes just darting from valley floor to sky, I knew exactly what this guy, the Seeker, meant. That we leave our homes, that we step through our doors to the world, that we travel our whole lives not because we want to collect exotic T-shirts, not because we want to consume foreign adventure the same Western way we consume plastic and

Styrofoam and LCD TVs and iPads, but because it has the power to renew us—not the guarantee, not the promise, just the possibility. Because there are places our imaginations can never construct for us, and there are people who we will never meet but we could and we might. It reminds us that there is always reason to begin again.

**The Lagarfljótsormur**
*Illustration © SiggaRún, 2013*

# Six

# Lake Monsters and Cute French Hitchhikers

Iceland has a mythical lake creature akin to Scotland's Loch Ness Monster called the Lagarfljót worm. After we left Seyðisfjörður and descended into Egilsstaðir, we decided to drive all the way around Lagarfljót in case the monster decided to make an appearance.

With sightings dating back as early as 1345 and as recent as February 2012, this worm monster ain't no fucking joke. There is even—ahem—a YouTube video of it. I'm not shitting you. Go look it up. Google "Iceland worm monster" and it will be the first hit. A sheep farmer drinking his morning coffee spotted the creature from a window, recorded it for a few minutes, and took the video to the news station in Egilsstaðir. Now admittedly, the video does look like a stationary bit of debris being pushed around by the current in icy, snow-covered water, but it also doesn't not look like it might not not be a monster.

Lagarfljót is a glacial finger lake with Iceland's "most important forest" surrounding its banks. Heavy siltation gives the water poor visibility (every lake with a lake monster conveniently has poor visibility), but sightings of the creature suggest it's a serpentine, humped beast that's either a few feet long, as long as a football field, or as long as the lake itself, depending on how drunk you are when you see it. In 1998, a schoolteacher and group of students claimed they saw it. Back in 1963 the head of the Icelandic National Forest Service claimed he saw it. In 1983, a contractor laying a thick telephone wire across the lake encountered something in the water that didn't like the cable, and when he pulled it out of the water, his crew found severe damage to the cable in 22 places. He told a Reykjavík newspaper, "I believe we dragged the cable directly over the belly of the beast. Unless it was through its mouth."

Sure, you can believe that methane gas, seeping up from fissures beneath the lake could send up material that might trick the eye, but we all know what happens to the asshole who offers that explanation in the movie, which is that he gets eaten by the huge fucking worm monster.

First of all, I refuse to be that guy. Secondly, I used to love all this cryptozoological shit when I was a kid. To the point where I read textbooks about unexplained phenomena from Bigfoot to the Big Bird of Texas well into middle school.

[However, because I was a savvy operator with the ladies, I never went on and on about the Chupacabra, the gigantic, man-eating Wuhnan Toads of China's isolated Hubei province, or the Goatman of Prince George's County, Maryland where sightings first began in Forestville and Upper Marlboro roughly around 1957. Unless she brought it up first, of course.]

As we drove by the lake, I explained my nostalgic predisposition to believing there are certain creatures hiding out in remote corners of the world still waiting to be discovered, hopefully before we wreck the planet and send them rocketing toward extinction as we're doing with everything else.

"Look at the Yeti," I said. "There was an international team of scientists who think they've found pretty incontrovertible evidence of some kind of unclassified ape living in remote parts of the Himalayas. We think the whole world is covered in McDonald's now, but I'm telling you there are still places where science has not been able to reach yet."

"Is that true?" said Bojo. "The Yeti? Really?"

"Yeah," said Trin. "Really?"

"Fuck yeah, look it up!" I said. "All I'm saying is that the test for all of these supposed creatures is that if they exist, we're about to find out about them. Everyone has a video camera on their phones now, accessible at a moment's notice. Everyone has an email or Facebook account to transmit that image instantly."

"Even the Yeti has one," said Trin optimistically. "Although his Facebook page is still the picture of the anonymous blue guy."

**[So when I got back to 'Merica, I finally did look up, for purposes of this book, the "evidence" of the Yeti discovered by the international team of scientists. Well, it turns out that scientists claiming they were 95% sure they'd found evidence of the Yeti turned out to be 100% some Russian government minister trying to stir up publicity. Sigh. At least I'll always have the Goatman of Maryland.]**

**Inside Joke #99:** We stayed in Höfn (which we pronounced "Hoffen") that night in the southeast corner of Iceland with the massive

Vatnajökull glacier within our sights. We vacillated back and forth about getting lobster because Höfn was supposedly famous for its lobster, but lobster also cost more than our stay in the hostel, so we opted for shitty ham-and-cheese sandwiches and soup instead. As we were deciding, though, Bojo said, "I don't know, how hungry are you guys? Lobster won't be very filling."

"I had that snack, so I'm OK, but I'll do whatever you guys want to do," said Trin.

"What about you, Steve?"

"I don't know, man; I'm kinda starving. I need to satiate this hunger."

"Yeah, I could go for satiating my hunger, too."

"I know, Boj. You and I are always on the same tummy schedule."

"What? No—" He started laughing. "Don't ever call it a 'tummy schedule.' Not ever again."

"Aw c'mon, man," I said, patting his shoulder. "We're tummy brothers. Tummy schedules unite!"

And from that point forward we never talked about a meal without referring to our tummy schedules.

It's possible you had to be there.

**Inside Joke #106:** Who did we see at this overpriced restaurant in Höfn but our old friends from Akureyri, Charlotte and Myriam-Sophie. We smiled and waved as we walked in, and they returned our greeting. By the time we'd finished our meals of soup and sandwiches that were way more bread than ham and cheese, however, our tummy schedules were still telling us eating time wasn't over. That's when I noticed that Myriam-Sophie had pushed aside half her burger and an entire plate of fries.

"It's just sitting there," I said. "I think she's going to throw it out."

"That sucks," said Trin.

"I can't let that happen." I got up and made my way over to the two French-Canadian girls. "Hey, guys!" I said, crouching down so that I wouldn't hover over them. I started asking them how their trip was going, where they were headed next, and boy, wasn't it crazy how we kept running into each other?

"Oh, and how'd you guys like the food here? Pretty great, right?"

"Eh, not so much," said Myriam-Sophie, pointing to her mostly full plate.

"What?" I said incredulously. "You don't like the fries? You're taking that with you, right?"

She shook her head vigorously. "No, it was not—uh—it was not very good."

"Well, can we have it?" I asked.

And at this both Myriam-Sophie and Charlotte erupted in giggles. Some of the other people in the restaurant turned to look.

"You want her, uh, her, uh," said Charlotte, whose English was a little rougher. "You want her bad food?"

"Sure!" I said. "We shouldn't let it go to waste."

Myriam-Sophie was covering her mouth and giggling like this was the craziest thing anyone had ever asked her, like, *Oh my God, you silly Americans! You'll eat anything!*

[And she hadn't even seen me in my element. If I'm reasonably drunk at a restaurant and someone leaves a plate of anything but garnishes, there's a pretty good chance I'll house it down before the bus boy even realizes the patrons have stood up and turned their backs. Hell, even if I'm not drunk. What I'm saying is if you eat with me keep your arms wrapped around your plate like concertina wire.]

After I'd thanked her and taken her plate back to our table and after we'd paid and departed, waving at a still tittering Charlotte and Myriam-Sophie and after we were back in the car, Bojo had the biggest shit-eating grin on his face.

"What?" I asked.

"Nothing, man. Those girls."

"What?"

"The way they were laughing. That satiated my hunger for cuteness."

For some reason this phrase totally stuck. To this day, a girl will do something in front of me, and I'll think psychically at Bojo, *That totally just satiated my hunger for cuteness.* Who will then, I bet, think psychically back at me, *Steve, one day please record me while I'm sleeping.*

## Hitching

At the hostel while Boj, Trin, and I hung out in the common area, two French girls—not French-Canadian, that's important—came up to us and asked if we could give them a ride west the next day. We said yes, and this is amusing for one reason alone.

Back in Akureyri before we'd headed out for the night, Bojo and I were sipping a couple beers and talking to two American dudes who were hitchhiking instead of driving. Both were nice guys, and one was even from Chicago and semi-recognized me from RedEye.

**[What an icon I am. Someone give me custody of Suri just for being badder-assed than either half of TomKat.]**

During the course of our conversation, however, they were clearly probing to see what kind of car we had so we could maybe give them a ride the next day if we could fit their gear, and in fact we passed them on our way out of town in the morning, standing by the side of the road with their enormous packs between their legs, thumbs extended.

This led Bojo and I to discuss how we found the act of hitchhiking around Iceland a kind of weirdly bourgeois thing to do.

"Like it's too dangerous and illegal to hitchhike in America, so American kids hop over here to have their faux-Kerouacian experience," I said.

"There's just something very 'look at me' about how they present it," he said. "You're hitchhiking, that's fine, that's great. Just don't expect me to be impressed."

"You're essentially a moocher. You're a First-World kid who had enough money to buy a plane ticket over to Iceland, so one presumes you have enough money to rent a car, but you're letting us bear the cost of your gas and transportation because you want to be able to go home and tell your friends, 'I hitchhiked around Iceland, brah! No big deal, just doing some hitchhiking. Never know who's gonna pick you up! Mlah mlah mlah!'"

"Doing it for the ability to say they did it rather than just taking a bus, which let's face it, there's basically only one road in Iceland, so they could do that pretty easily."

"Yeah, for real. Fuck those guys."

We went on in this vein for 20 minutes.

*Weeeellll* it turns out if two pretty French girls ask you for a ride instead of two lanky Americans, your opinion of hitchhiking improves dramatically. Suddenly you'll discard whole boxes of presents intended for your family as well as much-needed medicine like insulin in order to cram the two of them into your i20.

Such was the case with Muriel and Ombeline, two tall, striking girls from Paris for whom we sat like chickens in factory farm cages for two hours so we could listen to their French accents. It is a well-worn truism that a French accent on a female is one of the most beautiful sounds to ever occur on our planet. Everything they say is beautiful. If a French girl says, "I want to lance this ass-boil and use the puss as a coating for a rotten hard-boiled egg that I'm going to eat via enema," it sounds wonderful and poetic and makes me want to touch her face and kiss her neck gently.

However, because I was in the front seat, it was too difficult to kiss anyone's neck gently, so instead we played Would You Rather.

My question [pointing to a small Icelandic town of maybe 150 as we drove by]: "Would you rather live in that town for the rest of your life and you could never leave *or* you can travel anywhere in the world you want, just living your life the way you do now, but you have to take a sheep with you. You have to take care of this sheep, arrange for its food, its medicine, its transportation, and whenever it dies you just get a new sheep that becomes your responsibility."

Their question [after discussing it in French for 10 minutes]: "Would you rather live in that town your whole life *or* you can travel but you have to be in a man pornography."

**[We assumed that "man pornography" meant what we thought it meant.]**

# SEVEN

# In the Twilight of the Glaciers

We dropped Muriel and Ombeline off at Skaftafell National Park where we'd scheduled a glacier walk.

**[In saying goodbye to Muriel, I hugged her and she said, "Oh, Americans say goodbye so strange." I apologized, went in to hug Ombeline, and she stopped me. She said, "No, like French." Then she did the double kiss thing with our cheeks touching, and maybe it was just because of her incredible accent and the fact that I hadn't touched a girl in several weeks and she smelled vaguely of flowers growing in Heaven, but when she pulled away I got all dizzy and pubescent.]**

If you've never seen a glacier, I highly recommend you make it your next outdoor vacation. I know, you're probably saying, "A glacier? Why? Who cares? It's just snow and ice, right?"

I'm something of a glacier nerd, so allow me to explain: Glaciers are fucking cool. Glaciers are hydrology and beauty and timespans that are impossible to conceive. They create rivers and lakes and drinking water. They are vast landscapes of pristine white that look like a block of the world went missing, whited-out by an editor. They carve, they flatten, and they shape the world. I remember in seventh grade learning about the geography of Ohio, how during the last ice age the glaciers came blasting down from Canada and flattened the land where I lived but stopped somewhere in the middle of the state, only to melt, all that water draining down and carving apart the rest. Every time we drove through the southern part of the state on my way to basketball scrimmages and whatnot I'd look at the tumbling hills and think of the water pushing through, draining down to Kentucky and beyond, even as the source retreated north to form the Great Lakes.

In addition to having a glacier named after a supposed double-amputee who scaled it (Eiríksjökull, to the west) Iceland happens to be home to the largest glacier by volume in all of Europe. The Vatnajökull (which boringly translates to "Water Glacier") ice cap covers 8,100 kilometers, which is 8 percent of the entire country. It's the star of a James Bond film and a key part of the second season of *Game of Thrones*.

Before traveling to Iceland, I'd written the following for RedEye:

> In case you hadn't heard—since it's been all over upwards of one of the blogs on this site—I'm going to Iceland for a while, and in trying to get an idea of what I want to see on my trip, I've decided some glaciers are a must. And lucky you, now you can prepare for a long blog post on glaciers! Hope you've got your seventh-grade science class notes handy.

You figure that with any extended vacation, you gotta see some nature and shit.

Nature and shit is the best, especially for city-dwellers, and especially for Chicagoans where if you want to actually get out and see anything decent you must first hop over the endless, mesmerizing suburban sprawl of the Chicagoland area, which has more concrete lots, car dealers, and tract-housing per capita than anywhere else on the planet (note: not a researched fact).

With Iceland's volcanic topography, history of environmental degradation by early human settlers, and sprawling glaciers, I'm assuming it will look not like Aurora, Illinois, and I'm greatly looking forward to this.

The reason you must go see glaciers in your lifetime is because they are all going away. According to the World Glacial Monitoring Service, 90 percent of the world's glaciers are in retreat, which sucks because many of these glaciers provide drinking water to millions of people from mainland Europe to Peru to Pakistan.

Iceland happens to be home to the largest ice cap in all of Europe, called Vatnajokull (there's supposed to be some dots in there or whatever, but this blog is for 'Mericans, not Frenchies). With a thickness of up to 1,000 feet, the glacier is named after Count Vatnajokull, who freed the merman from the clutches of the Greenland Norse and brought peace to the internecine conflict of the Seventh Order of the Mermanic Empire (note: also not a researched fact, existence of merman still in scientific dispute).

Vatnajokull has been having some problems recently. Scientists have found that ice-marginal lakes in front of outlet glaciers have been expanding rapidly since 1995. This is important because as researcher Anders Schomacker of the Institute of Earth Sciences at the University of Iceland wrote, the development of "land-based glacier termini" into "lake-terminating glaciers is an eye-catching environmental change."

And here's where it gets weird: When we think of global climate change, we think of different things depending on our level of sophistication with the subject. Some assume that planetary warming means across-the-board warmer temperatures without variation. This is not the case. Warming will cause all kinds of weird weather, including heavy snowstorms during the winter. However, even if you're more familiar with the subject, you might not know that scientists are beginning to think that global warming will eventually lead to more earthquakes and volcanic eruptions.

"Huh?" I hear you saying. "Is this like the Mermanic Tribes of the Great Labrador Current? Not really a researched thing?"

Unfortunately, it is a thing.

Glaciers exude enormous, unthinkable pressure upon the land on which they rest. Rapid melting will reduce this weight not in incremental easing as in most historic periods of glacial retreat, but more like jerking a bag of cement off a spring-loaded platform. Tectonic instability results, and the likelihood of volcanic eruptions rises. Iceland, with 10 percent of its land mass covered by glaciers and a hotbed of volcanic activity, could be dealing with a spike in eruptions similar to Eyjafjallajokull (not a made-up fact; they actually name stuff that way), which you'll recall grounded air traffic across Europe in 2009.

So see all the glaciers you can while you can because even if you still don't think anthropogenic climate change is real, the merman will undoubtedly want revenge soon for being banished to the Svallbard Undersea Empire of the Damned (not a researched fact: Svalbard may in fact be spelled with one "L").

As warned by the incredibly informative Reykjavík video store clerk, we were sure to go on a guided tour because every year there are tourists who decide to hike a glacier by themselves and end up getting killed when they fall into a crevasse. For a glacier walk, you have to strap on crampons. I thought everyone knew what a crampon was until I met Bojo and Trin, but they didn't, so I won't assume you do: A crampon is like an ice-shoe. You strap it to your boots, and it has little spikes that stick in the ice and make it easy to traverse icy surfaces. I used them when I climbed a mountain in Wyoming. Now that you know what a crampon is, try to bring it up in casual conversation. It will make people feel like pussies.

Anyway, I should note that this was not exactly a death-defying hike we were on. Our group included tweens and elderly women whose hips looked like they were about ready to go flying out of their sockets. Our walk took us over Skaftafell, an outlet glacier of Vatnajökull.

**[An outlet glacier is like the finger of a hand. It's part of the larger ice cap that comes riding into valleys below the larger mass of compacted**

**ice and snow. (Oh my fuck, did this aside only have actual useful information?)]**

Our tour guide introduced himself as, "Dah-nee. Don-ee? Danny?" and over the course of two hours we hiked from the glacier's terminating point up over the ridges of ice, still black in places with the ash of volcanic debris. Skaftafell—and other outlet glaciers—looks kind of like the ridges of a deformed potato chip, as all that ice and snow melts and reforms seasonally. They are also pocked with holes, caves, and canyons because as the water melts it flows towards the weakest points. Dah-nee. Don-ee? Danny? at one point led us, one at a time, down into one of these tunnels, each of the 15 of us handing off our cameras to get a picture of the person peering down into this cave of ice before carefully cramponing our way back up to level ground. I kept gazing up at the massive ramp of ice that led up the valley to Vatnajökull. From our spot at the very bottom, the ice cap looked bigger than the sky. It seemed impregnable, immovable, and indissoluble by time or space or God. If only this were the case.

The other reason you should go see a glacier soon is because they are being wiped off the face of the earth by our rapidly warming planet. Occasionally, climate change denialists will point to a glacier here or there that is growing, but as noted, 90 percent of the world's glaciers are retreating. Not to get all sciencey on you, but the World Glacier Monitoring Service has found that this retreat began basically when we started burning large amounts of fossil fuels and that since 1975, glacial retreat has accelerated beyond anything scientists predicted back in the '70s. The latest data shows that the loss of glacial mass from the decade long period of 1996 to 2005 is *double* the rate of loss from 1986 to 1995 and *four motherfucking times* the rate of loss that glaciers experienced from 1976 to 1985. Vatnajökull has lost somewhere in the neighborhood of 235 square miles since 1958.

This is extremely unsettling to say the least because glaciers, in addition to giving Steve Markley a boner, supply drinking water for literally hundreds of millions of people all over the world.

We could see where the Skaftafell glacier had pushed rock and sand and silt into a massive pile at its tip and how far it had retreated since. Unfortunately, Dah-nee. Don-ee? Danny? and I did not see eye-to-eye on what this meant.

"It has happened before," he said. "Sometimes the glaciers are retreating, sometimes they are growing. When the Vikings first came here the glaciers were much smaller. So maybe it is global warming, but maybe it's just natural cycles, and the glacier will grow again. Nobody really knows."

Not to get into a whole big thing here (I mean, at some point I do want to get back to telling stories about chicks, terrifying ducks, and Trin's poops), but this is perhaps the most unsettling argument people present about why global warming is not a problem because it assumes that all the thousands and thousands and thousands of scientists who have been studying global climate for 40 fucking years never once stopped and asked, "Y'uk, y'uk—I wonder if the Earth's ever warmed before?! I know! Maybe we should check to see just in case that's what's happening now instead of this funny story we made up about cars causing it!"

Dah-nee. Don-ee? Danny? kept repeating this line of thought, however, and when I told him that it's well-documented that glacier loss has been accelerating since the 1970s he said he'd never heard of that.

*Be cool, baby,* I told myself, petting my own argumentative nature. *No point in getting into a dispute with your glacier tour guide. Save the ammo, baby. Keep your powder dry.*

**[I'm not sure why I talk to myself like a pervert.]**

All this is how I ended up in a polite email fight with an Icelandic glaciologist.

Before I left I made contact with some actual Icelandic scientists who study the country's glaciers, one of whom was Anders Schomaker of the Earth Sciences Institute at the University of Iceland. Anders was the author of a paper called "Rapid expansion of marginal ice-contact lakes at the Vatnajökull ice cap." In this study, Schomaker described: "Outlet glaciers from the Vatnajökull ice cap in Iceland retreat rapidly and marginal ice-contact lakes are expanding fast. The switch from land-based glacier termini to glaciers terminating in lakes is a dramatic environmental change in the ongoing deglaciation. The large heat capacity of the ice-contact lakes and the change into calving glacier fronts accelerates the loss of ice from Vatnajökull."

In other words, them glaciers be melting fast.

Anders and I never managed to meet up, so instead I ended up in an email exchange with Skafti Brynjólfsson, a glacial geologist at the Icelandic Institute of Natural History.

Skafti partially works on small valley and cirque glaciers in the alpine landscape of middle north Iceland called the Tröllaskagi peninsula. He's also worked on projects both on Vatnajökull and the Hofsjökull ice cap. He and his colleagues monitor changes in glaciers with connections to changes in the weather, measuring mass balance by drilling stakes into the ice to check out winter accumulation of snow pits and summer ablation. This is useful for monitoring the effects of small-scale weather events alongside the extensive glacial monitoring taking place all over Iceland—especially because "small valley and cirque glaciers are considered extremely sensitive to small changes of the climate."

**["Hey Markley, if you don't stop talking about this science bullshit I'm going to switch to Tucker Max's book because at least that guy understands he's a fucking idiot."]**

Skafti's larger project takes him to the Drangajökull ice cap in northwest Iceland to focus on glacial geology, to map and model the glacial history of the ice cap in those last 12,000 years. This has a lot to do with mapping landforms and moraines in an attempt to reconstruct the glacier's storied past.

He travels to Iceland's hinterlands for three to five weeks at a time where he lives in a base camp with a small team of scientists eating dry and canned food. Some days they spend the morning hiking two hours to their work site.

"We log the sediments, sketch up all structure in the sections, which can tell us how the landform was formed, sample organic material and tephra for [carbon-14] dating to get the exact age of landforms," he wrote to me. Other days they hike 20-25 kilometers to explore and map new areas.

Skafti described the retreat of Iceland's glaciers.

"The big glaciers in south and middle Iceland are receding fastest, up to 100 meters per year. It's common that these glaciers retreat tens of meters per year (30-50 meters). The small glaciers in middle north Iceland retreat slower (0-15 meters per year). Their ablation area is situated about 700-900 meters above sea level compared to 50-500 [for the glaciers] in south. The Drangajökull ice cap in northwest Iceland is retreating slowly, on average a few meters per year. Some years it has gained mass and increased a little bit. It is colder in the Drangajökull area and less ablation [occurs] during the summer compared to the south and central highlands. Some of the small glaciers in the central highlands and west Iceland are disappearing and in fact one, called Ok, disappeared a few years ago."

It's difficult to compare glaciers in different parts of the world because glaciers don't just ablate because of the heat but can also grow with increased precipitation. According to Skafti, Iceland's glaciers have behaved much like those in the rest of the North Atlantic, such as those in Norway and Svalbard, in that they were actually growing for a short period from 1970 to 1995 but have been in retreat since.

I ask him if recession of Vatnajökull is particularly troubling since it's also on top of so many volcanoes.

"Not yet," he replied. "But scientists expect the activity of the volcanoes to increase when the ice mass [Vatnajökull] becomes thinner and lighter. The pressure on the volcanoes will be less and eruptions could become more common in the next decades and centuries. Seismic activity could increase in connection to more active volcanoes, but it is not likely to be problematic. Increased volcanic activity can be a problem, especially because of ash fall that can be troubling for many of our daily activities."

The melting glaciers could have other impacts as well.

"Glaciers are [an] important water source for hydropower plants in Iceland. Summer melting is expected to be high in the next 40 to 70 years with high water discharge to the dams. After that the discharge will become gradually less as the glaciers decrease. When [a] glacier becomes considerably smaller there will be little ice to melt over the summer months to fill up the dams . . . This could be a problem for electricity production in the future."

However, Skafti repeated Danny's idea that the melting glaciers could come back, even that we could have another ice age soon. He wrote, "I don't want to say anything about when we can expect a new ice age, but in the 'recent' geological history the warm periods have lasted ten or [a] few tens of thousands of years. The present warm period has lasted for about 10,000 years now, so who knows …?"

I wrote back to him, "From what I'm familiar with about anthropogenic climate change, we have made it virtually impossible to enter another ice age, that the amount of $CO_2$, methane, and other greenhouse gases we have released/continue to release will guarantee further warming for quite some time."

"Yes, I don't want to say much about this because I am not a specialist on this topic," he wrote back. "I have never worked with this and have only been reading some papers and discussing this with friends and colleagues."

I enjoyed this exchange with Skafti and made him promise that if I made it back to Iceland he would let me hang out on a glacier with his team and do glaciery things. I'd also take the time to drop some knowledge about the growing indicators of the serious threat posed by climate change and that cyclical explanations such as solar radiation had long been reduced to the wishful thinking of petroleum geologists. This was, after all, the summer of 2012: The year when the world burned, when drought plagued every continent and drove food prices to spectacular heights, when 94% of the Greenland ice sheet experienced a flash melting event, when a new study by Joseph M. Prospero, Joanna E. Bullard and Richard Hodgkins linked massive dust storms sweeping off the southern coast of Iceland to the country's melting glaciers following glacial outburst floods, when the satellite system GRACE (Gravity Recovery and Climate Experiment) determined that just the ice melt from 2003 to 2010 had produced a volume of water that would cover the entire United States up to 18 inches, most of it coming from just to Iceland's north in Antarctica and Greenland.

Or maybe I'm just such an asshole and have no problem yelling at an Icelandic glaciologist about what's fucking with his ice masses. At least I got to stand on that big, beautiful, white bastard in case it turns out I'm right. See you in hell, glaciers.

# EIGHT

# The Comedian Mayor

Jón Gnarr was Iceland's most famous comedian—think of him as the Sacha Baron Cohen meets Jon Stewart meets young Robin Williams of the country of 318,000—until the 2008 financial crisis collapsed not only the Icelandic economy but the citizens' faith in the major political parties. On a lark, Gnarr formed the Best Party, a band of poets, punks, and pop musicians, and ran for mayor of Reykjavík. The Best Party's platform included bringing a polar bear to the zoo, free towels at all public pools, a drug-free parliament within 10 years, and a promise to break all of its promises. Gnarr swore he would not form a coalition government with anyone who hadn't seen all five seasons of the classic HBO series *The Wire*. His official campaign slogan (or as official as anything got for the Best Party) was, "Hooray for all kinds of things!"

Oh, and he won.

"No one has to be afraid of the Best Party," he said in his acceptance speech. "Because it is the best party. If it wasn't, it would be called the Worst Party or the Bad Party. We would never work with a party like that."

Now two years into a four-year term, Gnarr had become something of an international celebrity. He's the subject of the award-winning documentary film *Gnarr*, he frequently garners headlines for his irreverent, post-modern take on politics, and, perhaps most surprisingly, he's proved an effective, if controversial head of Iceland's capital. His story is remarkable, and I highly recommend the documentary chronicling his run.

I'm as surprised as you that I got an interview with the guy, but Bojo, Trin and I hustled back to Reykjavík after our glacier hike to meet with him. We got up the earliest we'd managed the entire trip and headed down to Reykjavík's City Hall. I told Gnarr's secretary that Trin was my videographer and Bojo my assistant. I sat down on the couch opposite him, and this is what happened (with a note to readers that this interview was previously published by the excellent online lit journal *The Rumpus*):

**[After greeting Mayor Gnarr and exchanging handshakes, my assistant and videographer set up and we all discussed the enormous Banksy print hanging above the mayoral desk. It is a black-and-white stencil of a handkerchief-wearing radical lobbing a would-be bomb actually composed of a colorful flower bouquet.]**

**Jón Gnarr:** He actually gave it to me.

**Me: So you know Banksy?**

No, I don't know him, but I got a message to Banksy, and I got a reply from this lady, who's supposed to be his spokesperson, and she said . . . I asked for this piece, and she wrote back and said that she had talked to Banksy and under the condition that it hang in the mayor's office . . .

And then I got it sent months later. Actually it was out of print, so we had to make a new—uh, draw a new flower bouquet, so if you compare this one to the original, they are different flowers . . . Very few people realize the uniqueness of this.

**[Gnarr speaks with the halting uncertainty of a person speaking in a second language. The Icelandic people all know English just well enough that they make very endearing mistakes, and when they stumble upon a place in their speech to use a well-worn American idiom, it comes out precise and robust ("skinned alive" being the best example in this conversation). Gnarr wears a suit and vest the color of beach sand with a blue undershirt and a skull ring smiles from his left ring finger. He sits with his legs crossed and takes his time articulating each answer. It should be noted that prior to sitting down with Gnarr, my companions and I had spent 10 days traveling across Iceland and Reykjavík. In asking about Gnarr, we mostly heard answers along the lines of, "It's a big joke. He will be gone soon." Yet for a man essentially known as a clown, Gnarr speaks with an undeniable gravity.]**

**So, you've been mayor for two years now, and I'm curious what you're most proud of and what's been your biggest disappointment or your biggest struggle.**

What I'm actually most proud of is still being here. [Laughs] Because this has been very challenging and very tough. And I'm very proud of this group of people that have joined me on this adventure, and us sticking together, and nobody giving up, nobody bailing out. So that we have managed to be here two years makes me very, very proud, and I think it's very important and unique because in the history of populist protest political parties they usually dissolve after the elections: "The campaign was fun but ..." And the weird thing is, us being chaotic and anarchical, we have brought stability to the city. And I have now been mayor longer than anyone since 2003 because of the political instability.

**[For much of its history, Reykjavík's municipal politics have been dominated by the center-right Independence Party, which became especially vulnerable after Iceland's financial crisis and its association with the bankers who thought they could turn a country less populous than certain dying Rust Belt towns into a financial superpower. The Best Party formed its coalition with the Social Democratic Alliance, a center-left umbrella group. While Americans like to complain about their two-party system, the Icelandic often express dismay about their "chaotic" multiparty system with shifting coalitions that often dissolve and reform on whims, sleights, and ego trips.]**

**What have you found most difficult, most challenging?**

Probably the responsibility and all the information that I have to take in, things I have to understand, things that I'm honestly not interested in.

**Were you prepared for the mundane day-to-day slog of actually running a city? Because that's so different than the energy behind your campaign.**

No, I wasn't prepared for it at all.

**That's a very honest answer.**

I had no idea what I was getting into, and I think even many of my associates in the Best Party didn't realize, even, how little I knew . . . Because I've never followed politics . . . you know, except for when you change presidents, it's like, "Who is the president of the United States? Yeah, it's this guy now?" And I follow now. I know who is the president. I rarely knew who was prime minister here, and when people appeared on television as politicians explaining something I rarely knew who they were. So in the early campaign I was not aware that we were running for municipality. I thought we were running for parliamentary.

**So you didn't even know the position you were seeking?**

No, that was in the early beginning, and the things that come with the job I was not prepared for at all. Our biggest task when we started was starting to prepare the budget for the city. I had no idea.

**So you sat down with smart people and said, "Tell me about the budget?" What was your strategy?**

Well, my strategy from the beginning was admitting I know nothing.

**That's very—most politicians don't admit that.**

Yeah, I've noticed. So I admitted I didn't know the difference between a billion and a trillion . . . What's the difference again? *[Laughs]* So, yeah, I was beaten up.

[Though we didn't have time to get into the specifics in a 30-minute interview, Gnarr was understating the degree of basket-case-edness he and his party faced when they took over Reykjavík. Difficult budgetary decisions had to be made almost immediately, cutting the city's spending by 10%, which included laying off 70 staff members, tightening the city's bus services, and attempting to unwind the disaster that is Reykjavík Energy—a utility that went batshit crazy with "Viking ambition" and ended up with debts five times larger than the city budget. Lest you think Gnarr took this as a joke, during an award ceremony for a social worker, he began to weep, wondering aloud if he was slashing the kind of social services that helped him as a troubled teenager who dropped out of high school and took up sniffing glue.]

**Learning on the job . . . That's what you went in for.**

Yeah, but by admitting I didn't know anything I took a beating in the press and from professional politicians.

**Yeah, but that's what most politicians do: Not know anything and then pretend their way through it.**

Yeah, there was some interview with me on the news here on TV, on local TV here and I was asked some question and I said, "I just honestly don't know" and it was like a breakthrough or something. It was like the first time in the world—in the history of humanity—that a politician on television says that he doesn't know. I said,

"I can find out and I can call you later, *[Laughs]* or have someone call you who knows."

**Let me ask you about your campaign: You came to prominence as kind of an anti-politician, but watching some debates and interviews during the campaign—you know, at first you were just telling jokes, but you began to give these very eloquent and thoughtful answers about how the Icelandic political class had ignored the role of artists and anyone [not in finance] . . . Did you feel like your campaign kind of evolved as you began to rise in prominence or rise in the polls?**

Yeah, that's always touched me or affected me very deeply, that this respect for artists, especially from authority . . . like we are some second-class people. And there's always this discussion annually about support for the arts, why should we support art and so on. Iceland, we are tiny, we're so tiny, and many people around the world don't even know we exist, but we are globally known for art—and music especially—and that makes me very proud. You know I can go wherever, to Kuala Lumpur or wherever, and if somebody will ask me where I'm from and I say I'm from Iceland, they say, "Yeah, Björk." And that makes me very proud and that makes me proud to be an Icelandic artist. So when they started to say—you know our opponents—started to criticize us for just being a group of artists that really pissed me off. Maybe then I got more serious, just pointing [out] the obvious that we are a very artistic country and we should put emphasis on that. And then came the idea that, can artists enter politics? And that was serious.

**At what point during the campaign did you go, "Oh shit, I might actually win this."**

The last few days. Then we realized . . . It kind of dawned on me that this was going to happen. And I kind of panicked. "What am I getting into? And how many years is this again? *[Laughs]* Was it three or four? What? It's four years?!"

**Are there plans [for the Best Party] to go national? I also heard you were sending people overseas to Europe to talk about perhaps expanding it. Is there any truth to that?**

Well, there are some political parties or political movements that have certain similarities with us. For instance, the Pirate Party, and they are quite exciting. We've had some meetings and discussions, but I mean the Best Party is nonexistent. It doesn't exist. It has no members. It has no manifesto other than just nonsense. But the point is that by naming it the Best Party there is no such thing as the Best Party and never will be.

[The Pirate Party has its roots in hacker culture and espouses a typical left-leaning platform of universal health care and free education coupled with access to the Internet as a universal right and the proliferation of open content, freedom of information, and transparency. With members in multiple European countries and New Zealand, the Pirate Party has so far hit its zenith in Sweden's European Parliament Elections of 2009 when it received more than 7% of the vote.]

**Will you seek another term as mayor or try for higher office or is this a one-time deal?**

I'm definitely not going for any higher office than this. This is not more than I can handle, but this is more than enough. I don't know about a second term, I just haven't decided yet. Also, it's not just up to me because we are a group of people, and I feel a certain type of responsibility to these people because it was I who got them into this.

**Could a phenomenon like the Best Party or your candidacy happen in America? Because it seems like there was a very specific set of circumstances in Iceland that allowed you to sneak in and take this thing.**

**[A reminder of those circumstances brought up in Chapter Three: While Iceland's financial crisis had many similarities to our own, the Icelandic banks and political class bred their own kind of financial magical thinking. A nation of fisherman literally walked off their boats into high finance, leading to the fastest banking expansion in the world's history. At the peak, three private banks held assets 10 times the size of Iceland's GDP. People borrowed in foreign currencies as property values tripled and the stock market soared to nine times its previous size. When the reckoning came, it was a time of abject panic. Yet Iceland, of the world's many troubled First World economies, stands alone as one of the post-crisis success stories. It refused to pay foreign creditors, left the banks to fail, and returned to its economic roots. Ripple effects and painful choices remain, yet compared to the likes of Greece or Spain or Ireland it got off easy.]**

A lot of our success here is due to our naivety, and our Icelandic society is not as advanced as your society.

**What do you mean by that?**

It's kind of a Shire. Like hobbits. It's much more simpler here. Honestly I've thought about it; I've been asked and people have wondered, Can this happen? I don't think so. I think if someone like me tried to enter . . . they would be skinned alive. I think it's not possible. I've also wondered if for instance England—if some famous English comedian decided to go into politics. They have some good comedians that are political, controversial figures like Eddie Izzard. I've thought of if Eddie Izzard went in to politics . . . but they'd crucify him.

*[Gnarr's assistant interrupts to signal that time is running short.]*

**Do you think there's something about the nature of democratic systems . . . where very self-righteous, insufferable, self-important dickweed types end up winning office because that's what voters reward or tend to reward?**

It's a strange thing. People tend to favor the underdog, like in the movies we favor the underdog, but when it comes to voting, we vote for the bully. It's so strange. We trust the bully much better than we trust the underdog. Maybe it's in our nature, but it is so that all around the world there is this certain type that can succeed in politics and it's people who are—alpha types? Alpha types of people, very logical and determined and ruthless. So if we are going to change democracy we have to find ways to get different types of people to enter into politics. But the system is not like that now. You have to be the alpha type.

**Hey, we're from America.**

Yeah, you know all about it.

[In our follow-up conversation via email, Gnarr gave me his take on the Obama/Romney matchup of 2012. He wrote (with edits): *Your country is so huge, influential, and powerful [that] it affects a cute little country like Iceland in a massive way. We are pretty powerless compared to you. In 1941, we were occupied by your army :). I am a socialist so I prefer the Democrats to Republicans. I feel more secure when they are in charge. I hope Obama will win and the Democrats get a majority in the Senate. I fear Romney is a gun-loving, conservative Christian fanatic, with all the nonsense that follows. Maybe he's not? Hey, here's Rammstein:* He then linked to the YouTube video for Rammstein's "Amerika."]

**Let's talk about something more fun. You may or may not be aware that David Simon, the creator of *The Wire*, recently got in a huff because a website was bracketing his characters and putting them in tournaments against each other to see who the best character was. He didn't think the show was being taken very seriously. But that's OK because I think the "best character" question is kind of silly anyway. So my question—this is very important, it's going to inform a lot about you—is what is your favorite season of *The Wire* and why?**

Wow. That's uh …

**That's the heaviest question I've asked.**

*[Laughs]* What is my favorite season? . . . I don't know. I haven't given this thought for a long time . . . Can we get back to it?

**Yeah, think about that. I didn't realize that would be the toughest question.**

That was a really tough question, and I would really like to answer that in a very good way.

**OK, we'll come back to that . . . So now that you're Iceland's most famous comedian by quite a significant margin do you have any plans to tackle the U.S. cultural-media market? Maybe star in a reality show where you date an NBA basketball player?**

Well, uh . . .

**We also have shows where you eat bugs or sing duets with D-list celebrities who are washed up.**

Yeah, I've seen a lot of your shows. *[Laughs]*

**Hey, I didn't say we were proud of them.**

No, I'd given thought—when we had really tough times here, I went to Europe for a conference, and I thought about seeking political asylum *[Laughs]* to flee all this, but no, I haven't given it a thought.

**[To give you an idea, Gnarr's most prominent role was as the megalomaniacal Marxist Georg Bjarnfredarson, which spanned the TV series *The Night Shift*, *The Day Shift*, and *The Prison Shift* (the shows followed the same characters, but the Icelandic think of them as separate filmic entities, if that makes sense), finally culminating in the film *Mr. Bjarnfredarson*. Director Ragnar Bragason calls the series, "television**

tragedies masquerading as comedy." Gnarr also had a radio show in which he made crank calls to the CIA and FBI, asking if they'd found his lost wallet.]

**So your future is very up in the air right now. You don't have specific plans for after your term.**

No, it's day at a time. We like to say we're doing time in politics, and I don't think we have any hope of early release for good behavior, so it's day at a time.

*[The assistant again interrupts to make sure the mayor understands he has to be somewhere. To his credit, he points to his watch and says something in Icelandic, which seems to indicate "just a few more minutes."]*

**Polls persistently show that the Icelandic believe in elves that live in the lava rocks, so my question is, do you, and if so, how do we see them?**

No, I don't believe in them. But the elves for many are like representatives of nature, like the guardians of lava. *[Laughs]* I don't believe in them, and I don't think there is any scientific research that shows they exist. I think this comes from the time when this country was inhabited first by monks, by Irish monks . . . before the Vikings came. When the Vikings moved into a place they just kind of killed everybody who was there before them. And the monks knew that, and the monks were clever and the Vikings were not. So the monks hid and avoided the Vikings, and the Vikings assumed they were here alone. So maybe when they were walking around they'd see a strange creature lurking or running away and assume it was a ghost or something . . . I think it comes from that, but it was just monks running for their lives . . . *[Laughs]* According to legend, they disappear into the stones, and that was just a monk going down a crack.

**You said you have an American friend. We have yet to pronounce a single Icelandic word correctly in any context. Do you know any Americans who have successfully learned Icelandic, and if so what was the point of that endeavor?**

Well, there is—many autistic people have this ability to learn weird foreign languages, and I think I've heard of autistic Americans who have been obsessed about Icelandic and learned it and speak it fluently, and I've seen it done in interviews on television. I'm not really sure if they were autistic, but there was this high school kid somewhere in the States who spoke fluent Icelandic and had never been here before.

*[Gnarr's assistant interrupts for the third and final time.]*

*The Wire*, can I write it and send it to you? I'll write it.

**I'd love that. Absolutely. Do you have time for one last serious question: We're going to celebrate National Day, where would you direct young American guys to go in Reykjavík, and how late can we go to bed and not seem like wusses?**

Yah Yah Yah Yah . . . Probably city center in front of parliament, that's where everything is happening, where the most action is.

There are big celebrations around the center. You cannot go to sleep until at least after 3, but the party will still be going on.

*[As we begin to leave, we get caught up in a conversation about the Icelandic countryside, explaining to Gnarr we'd spent the previous week driving around the country in a rented car admiring the beauty of the land.]*

Do you know Doug Stanhope, the stand-up comedian?

**Yeah, sure.**

He was here last year. He wanted to meet me. And he was absolutely in love with [Iceland]. He's a . . . uh . . . peculiar person . . . I met him and took him to the maximum-security prison, and he did stand-up. He did stand-up for the prisoners. His first time sober doing stand-up—sober because he was not allowed to be intoxicated in the prison. Yeah, we had a great time. And he was so fascinated—people are fascinated by the harmlessness of this place . . . It's such a harmless place . . .

**I mean, people still hitchhike here. You don't see that in America.**

I had friends from France last summer and they were walking around and went to the main shopping street. And there they saw a lady with a baby carriage. And she parked the carriage outside the store and then went inside the store . . .

**We saw that today! On our way here.**

**[Literally on our walk to City Hall that morning we'd spotted a baby in a stroller outside a café playing with a chair. It was just sitting in its stroller—no adult in sight—slamming a folding chair around and scooting around in its seat like it wanted to roll down the hill. "Are you kidding?" Bojo said. "You'd get arrested for this back home."]**

And then she went inside the store and left it. And they had never seen this before. It's the harmlessness. It's a Shire. It's a hobbit town.

***

Less than a day after our conversation—perhaps after taking a few minutes to brush up on what happened in each season—Gnarr emailed me with his response to my question about *The Wire*. Appropriately enough, his answer revealed more about him than any of the other questions managed during the rest of the interview. Edited for print, here it is:

> *Hi Stephen*
>
> *I really liked our meeting this morning. It was a real pleasure meeting you guys. Your question on* The Wire *is probably the single most important question I've had from a journalist since I started this job.*
>
> *After careful thinking I would have to say I favour Season 4 the most in a professional and personal way. Key reasons are two: Education and literature or: Schools vs. creativity. I'm a dropout. I have no formal education and I'm very critical of the educational system in general.*
>
> *I'm a creative person. For me 4 [revolves] around [a] system vs. humanity/person. Deep? Makes sense? Goosebumps and*

*chills, mind-gripping like a book. I love television. It tought [sic] me everything before the Internet. My favorite characters are in the spotlight: Chris and Snoop as the odd couple and Omar, even though they have their best scenes in other seasons. When Snoop was killed I cried.*

**[This is incorrect because Snoop was killed in Season 5. Either he confused the seasons or it's possible he was referring to Bodie's death on a street corner, which happened at the end of Season 4, and is, in my mind, one of the most haunting deaths of any character in the entire series.]**

*Bottom line: In [Season] 4 television becomes literature. It's art.*

*Hope this is worth something :)*
*Jón Gnarr*
*-Anarchist, atheist and clown (according to a comment on a webpage).*

*A Silhouette of Halldór Laxness*
Illustration © SiggaRún, 2013

# NINE

# Independentish People

Icelanders are one of the most literate people on Earth, with the highest per-capita book sales of any country. At one point during this trip when we were back in Reykjavík, I walked into a bookstore, looked for the cute bookstore clerk (every corporate-owned bookstore has one) and asked her, "What's the Great Icelandic Novel?"

Without hesitation, she handed me a novel by prominent Icelandic author Halldór Laxness called *Independent People*. First published in two volumes in 1934 and 1935, it tells the story of Bjartur of Summerhouses, a cantankerous, hard-bitten sheep farmer, who wanders over plains and through blizzards muttering poetry and whose only goal in life is to be free of debt and live on his farm as a "self-standing folk" (he's kind of like an Icelandic Ron Swanson). His wives die; he raises another man's daughter as his own; and his children disappear to "a land even more remote, America, which is farther than death." Through it all, Bjartur stubbornly clings to the notion that a man's freedom is his only currency even as the notion proves fallacious again and again. Widely considered Laxness's greatest work, it was the cornerstone of his 1955 win for the Nobel Prize for literature—the only Icelander to do so. *Independent People* was actually out of print in English for 50 years, largely due to Laxness' perceived communist sympathies during the West's enduring Red Scare.

Upon cracking the novel, I immediately take to Bjartur and his unaware, no-nonsense manner that Laxness so sardonically uses to send up the very idea of "independence." Bjartur brims with wisdom.

Bjartur on talking to his dog: "No, I didn't think you would understand. You dogs are pretty poor objects really, though on the whole I think we humans have even less to boast about."

On women: "You women are more to be pitied than ordinary mortals, I suppose."

On books: "My dear Olafur, for goodness sake don't let anyone think that you take all that sort of thing seriously. You should beware of believing things you see in books. I never regard books as the truth, and least of all the Bible."

On Jesus: "Who saw Jesus rise on Sunday? A bunch of women, I expect, and how much can you rely on women and their nerves?"

On his dying newborn: "My tongue, you see, is more used to talking about lambs than human beings, and the idea was simply to ask you whether you didn't think it would be worthwhile pouring a few drops of warm milk down its throat to see if it can't be kept going till morning."

On his then revitalized infant daughter: "You can't really expect it to be much of a thing—the way mankind is such a sorry affair when you come to look at it as it actually is."

In a grocery store parking lot near Vík we spotted a small white van with colorful Chuck Norris graffiti adorning both sides. I pointed out to the guys that I had seen this same van in at least two other towns on this trip—a van with Chuck Norris's name in a teal emblem and his orange-haired, open-shirted visage on the sliding doors not being something you easily forget. We finally put it all together when we saw Charlotte and Myriam-Sophie in the store. This was the vehicle they had rented, a camper van where they crammed into a claustrophobic slot in the back, bundled into all their clothes, and actually slept during the cold nights. They showed us the inside, which had a week's worth of their clothes, food, sleeping bags, and garbage piled in the back. Even more Chuck Norris quotes plastered the interior. They explained that they had not wanted this particular camper, but the company that rented it to them seemed to think of it as the most treasured vehicle in their fleet. We invited them to eat at our hostel with us. While we cooked a truly pitiable meal of spaghetti with kidney beans, peas, and marinara sauce kind of jelled together into a soup, they told us their story: seeing the incredible northwestern fjords, getting hit on by every Icelandic man with whom they crossed paths, how they had first met studying abroad in Japan. Charlotte bemoaned her inability to express herself in English and Myriam-Sophie expounded on Montreal's student protests. After a while, it came out that Charlotte was actually the granddaughter of a guy named Charles Biddle and the daughter of a woman named

Joe Bocan. Charles Biddle, it turns out, was a pretty famous jazz bassist. Born in Philadelphia before immigrating to Montreal, he became a fixture of the Montreal Jazz scene.

**[And late in his life appeared in the Bruce Willis-Matthew Perry film _The Whole Nine Yards_, thus confirming my theory that no one should get to be known as a legend until they co-star with Bruce Willis and/ or Matthew Perry.]**

Joe Bocan, meanwhile, is a pretty famous Quebecoise actress and singer. Charlotte explained how when her grandfather came north from America during our long period of racial segregation, white and black jazz players appearing side-by-side on the stages of Montreal fascinated him. Joe met Biddle's son, Charles Biddle Jr., when she saw him playing in a club, and their partnership endured despite her family's extreme displeasure at the biracial relationship.

We ended up hanging out with the girls one more time in Reykjavík. We met up at a bar and went back to our apartment (after they made us promise _several times_ not to rape and murder them), where we stayed up talking until nearly 6 a.m.

Charlotte's story got me stuck trying to give expression to something I felt while I was in Iceland but never really figured out. Here's the best I can do to approximate what her story made me think of:

Iceland often gets credited as the world's "most feminist country." It had the first female head of state, Vigdís Finnbogadóttir, who served as president from 1980 to 1996, and now it has the first openly gay prime minister in Jóhanna Sigurðardóttir.

Electing a lesbian prime minister (not to mention a comedian mayor) seems to drive to the heart of the Icelandic's hyper-tolerant attitudes. One might think that a homogenous nation where the bloodlines are so pure people have to check and make sure they're not related before they date would lend its people a cultural or racial insensitivity, but this couldn't be further from the truth. In traveling to both Sweden and Iceland, it's funny how some of the least diverse countries now have the people who are seemingly the most untroubled by those not like them. Where immigrant-rich countries like the United States benefit enormously from the skills and determination of those immigrant generations arriving again and again, each wave is inevitably met with high degrees of xeno-phobia and hostility.

One might also shrug off the figurehead nature of a lesbian prime minister—"Good for you, give yourself a pat on the back for your tolerance, sure"—but Sigurðardóttir arrived with an aggres-sive agenda that included banning strip clubs from Iceland.

**[And less than a year after our trip, certain politicians began agitating for a ban on internet porn, which, with the internet is kind of like try-ing to ban cussing or oxygen or couples groping each other in public. Good luck.]**

As a First Amendment absolutist, I don't exactly agree with the decision (free expression also extends to the expression we don't like). However, I still find the empowered nature of Iceland's women extremely appealing. This is why Iceland is occasionally described as the world's most feminist country. In an age when the skills that made men the dominant sex for millennia (lifting things, swinging swords, etc.) are less important, it's easy to see how Iceland's attitudes about the role of the sexes will become the growing norm for civilization.

In this eventual easing of sexual and racial prejudices one can squint and almost see over the horizon to the day when a story like that of Joe Bocan and Charlie Biddle Jr. sounds as normal to an American as it does to a Pakistani as it does an Icelander. You can almost see to some vague but total integration of race, sex, and culture as the new normal, so that when two people from different backgrounds with different skin tones fall in love, no one, anywhere, notices. A time when the world internalizes the idea that the true "independence" of an open society is freedom from one's own fear of a supposed "other."

Or as Bjartur of Summerhouses might say, "Good, as long as nothing happens. Some people grumble about monotony—such complaints are the marks of immaturity; sensible people don't like things happening."

# TEN

# Blue Lagoon / Of Monsters and Men

### From "I Am the Worst: Blue Lagoon Edition"

So one of the things you're supposed to do while in Iceland is head about an hour south of Reykjavík to a natural hot springs called the Blue Lagoon. Enterprising Icelandic built a geothermal spa around this pool of natural bathwater and cleverly charge tourists double the price in the summer (somewhere in the neighborhood of $44) for admittance. Though we've been scrimping as much as we can—we had a very public rock, paper, scissors contest to see who got to eat the last hard-boiled egg—Trin, Bojo, and I decided this is just something you have to do if you visit Iceland, tourist trap or not.

Now pay attention: The way this works is the Blue Lagoon attendants give you a wrist bracelet at the door with some kind of supercomputer inside. This bracelet allows you to open and close a locker of your choice and purchase drinks at the hot-spring-side bar. What it doesn't allow you to do is pound Polar Bear beers inside the bathroom stall, which is more of a Steve Markley invention (and in fact superior to a supercomputer), Polar Bear being kind of the Pabst Blue Ribbon of Iceland. Once we breezed by the locker room signs demanding that we shower naked before entering the pool, we dipped our first toe into the Blue Lagoon. Here are some things I observed:

1) The air temperature is not warm, but the water is bathwater to really-hot-bathwater. This fell right into my vector of being uncomfortably hot or cold depending on whether I was standing or neck-deep wading, so already I kinda don't get the appeal.

2) They have this bullshit thing called a "silica mud mask," which are these pots of semen-colored goop that everyone is supposed to swim over to and immediately rub all over their faces without FDA examination or even a basic check for carcinogens. While I voiced these objections—"The Icelandic probably sit around laughing with each other about all the kinds of crazy semen-like goop they can get Americans to put on their faces." —Trin was already donning his silica mud mask in heavy handfuls.

"So refreshing," he said, looking like a pale imitation of one of those African tribesmen on NatGeo.

"Oh yeah, what does it do?" I challenged.

"I don't know, exfoliates or invigorates or something like that. Just put it on, Steve."

So there we floated for the next 10 minutes, just three cool American guys in their whiteface silica mud masks.

3) After removing our mud masks via waterfall, I had to towel off and return all the way upstairs to slam another Polar Bear beer (wouldn't a better name be "Polar Beer"? Maybe that is what it is and I was getting tipsy). The architects of the Blue Lagoon did not take into consideration how difficult it would be for kids from Ohio on a budget to escape paying for overpriced beer when they designed the place. I'd prefer if the Blue Lagoon were more like the community pool in Mount Vernon, Ohio, where kids just stepped behind the nearest tree and then lobbed the aluminum into the bushes. God bless America.

4) We watched the lifeguard—one of the only black guys we've seen in the country, with a physique like Adonis got a little carried away with the abs workout (what? so I noticed, so what?)—drill future lifeguards in strapping people to those orange stretchers and carrying them out of the water to safety. This became our entertainment for the next half-hour as we waited for the carrying-turns to come back around to the blond female trainee. For some reason, however, there were also old people involved in this training, some of whom had dimensions of fleshial droop that made them not only poor orange stretcher carriers, but also kind of aesthetically disturbing because of the pruney way warm water acts on skin. Bojo seemed to like it, though, and couldn't stand up for the entire half-hour.

5) We tried the sauna over my objections. If I wanted to be super-uncomfortably hot, I'd watch a chiseled black lifeguard hoist fake-injured people out of the water like a normal person. Obviously, saunas attract all kinds of sickos, and the moment we sat down, we were basically

making room for a flirting coed contingent of 75-year-old German perverts. Trin stayed for like an hour.

6) Back out in the geothermal pool, I realized hot-springs drunk is even worse than hot-tub drunk. It felt like we were moving through molasses, and both Trin and I commented how it would be nice to just fall asleep. Instead, this happened:

7) I'd noticed this youngish girl noticing me, who then noticed me noticing her, but this was not a situation where I particularly wanted to make conversation, given that I felt like the hot water had turned my drunk into some kind of Native American spirit-walk stoned-ness. Some older, balder, tattooed gentleman, though, was following her around so I felt a certain obligation to allow her to rescue herself by striking up conversation. She appeared to be roughly 18.2 years old and had what looked like either a tattoo or a very waterproof henna thing in the center of her forehead—a big dot surrounded by four little dots. I never asked about this. What I did ask was where she was from, which it turns out was Kansas City. Apparently, this young lady was a Wiccan Girl Scout— and by this I mean she was a practicing Wiccan who also happened to be a Girl Scout, not that there is a separate branch of the Girl Scouts catering to Wiccans. She was in Reykjavík on an ambassador mission for the Scouts but was more interested in getting laid. Lest you think I'm exaggerating the forwardness of this Wiccan Girl Scout's conversational tactics, Trin and Bojo soon appeared in the pool behind me, and I kind of drunkenly slithered over the berm separating us, thinking I could just call out to my friends and make my escape, at which point the

Wiccan Girl Scout simply made her way around the side where she proceeded to tell us that we were the sexiest guys in the pool and she and her Girl Scout ambassador troupe had been giggling at us previously. Said troupe then waded by very opportunistically and she waved and called out to them and explained that they were afraid of us. "We're not like in the Girl Scouts," she explained at what I can only assume was my evident discomfort and near-hallucinatory buzz. "I mean, we are, but we're older. I'm in nursing school."

"A nursing school Wiccan Girl Scout," I said. "Sure. Just like my last five girlfriends."

8) Not long after this, we looked at our fingers, which looked like cooked white raisins and decided that the Blue Lagoon on a Wednesday afternoon was the equivalent of going to bingo night at a rest home on Bring Your Sexually Precocious Granddaughter Day. We went to shower naked with each other.

9) The fallout from the Blue Lagoon, just to warn you, includes your skin feeling like it's coated in ash, finding flakes of silica mud mask still clinging to earlobes and errant crevasses of your face while you wonder how many Blue Lagoon teenage male employees manage to masturbate into the concoction before it hits poolside, and if you drank even the moderate amount that I did, the sensation that your soul has left your body and is riding six feet above you, looking down, shaking its head and muttering darkly.

Oh, and I got my interview with the mayor of Reykjavík that morning. Guess I shoulda led with that.

## From "We're Staying in Of Monsters and Men's Old Apartment"

After a promising interaction with the publicist for the band Of Monsters and Men, I'm sorry to report that I haven't heard back from the woman now that I'm in-country. In a bizarre coincidence, however, we are now actually staying in the band's old apartment just north of the city center.

After tiring of hostels where we slept 37 to a room and Bojo's tectonic-plates-subducting-sounding snoring kept everyone awake (except for Bojo) and Bojo and Trin got caught multiple times lathering each other's backs with soothing lotion after we all got sunburned at the Blue Lagoon and my morning erection evolved from "manageable inconvenience" to "madness-inducing priapism" and the National Coalition of Icelandic Hostels sent a letter to Trin asking him to please take it easy on their toilets because apparently he processes food like Paul Bunyan after eating an entire fibrous evergreen forest, we decided to relocate to an Airbnb.com apartment for our last days in Reykjavík.

And yeah, not only is this where the band used to live, it's also where they filmed the music video for their hit single "Little Talks." The walls remain decorated with their artwork, including a wolf with colorful feathers and a yellow nose howling at the ceiling and some kind of stick-legged elephant spouting oil from its trunk—the oil crawling up over the bathroom door and scrawled with gold-and-silver graffiti. The band also left their names written above their rooms, and we assume the word "fokkingz" means approximately what it does stateside, those potty-mouthed rock stars.

While this seems like an enormous coincidence, it's really not, since any famous Icelander apparently knows all the other Icelanders in vaguely personal ways. You could never play Six Degrees of Kevin Bacon here (with Kevinjum Baconjdarger, I presume?) because you'd start and then just figure out whomever you were talking to knew the guy. Or his sister would work with the famous person at the hospital or their fathers would be golfing buddies.

In fact, Iceland even has what I've come to describe as "Incest Facebook," which is a government website where people can look up potential dates and hookups to find out if their children would be born with 11 fingers. Part of the brilliance of being some American guy going up to a female in a bar is that they don't have to check their Incest Facebook app because all our incest is at least four generations behind us (so we know that Bojo and Trin's back-lotioning time is totally fine).

As for Of Monsters and Men, they had clearly passed Peak Plead, but I thought I might be able to sneak an interview with them anyway ("Peak Plead" being a term I invented and used mostly in my head back when I was interviewing bands and musicians a lot; they are basically the most wretchedly aggressive self-promoting artists who will beg, cajole, and weep for you to write them up in any kind of music venue in any significant way right up until the moment they realize they've gotten famous, at which point music writers are of as much interest and use to them as conch shells superglued to a business suit [which is to say, ridiculous and useless to the point where it's almost annoying to think about such a thing]; by the way, this is not an indictment of any particular musician, especially of Of Monsters and Men, who are probably very nice people judging from the way basically all the Icelandic are, but think of any struggling musician you know, and then think of how all famous musicians behave, and tell me I'm not right).

Now the main reason I want to interview Of Monsters and Men is to find out how they had all those people sharing this lackluster low-flow toilet because it's barely keeping up with Trin alone right now.

After this posted, I received the following annoyed email from OMAM's publicist:

*Hey Stephen, just saw your write up.*

*I'm actually the band's manager, not publicist. And the reason you have not been able to get an interview is not because the band has passed "Peak Plead" but because they have had only a few days of off time before they leave the country for months. They have very limited time with their families and loved ones. And at some point, they need some "time off" like all of us. They also had a last-minute trip to Germany while you were here to play a halftime show at the Euro Soccer Championships.*

*I'm sorry that it didn't work out but hopefully this helps you to understand that it's not about a lack of gratitude, just time, which is something else that gets lost when things get busy for bands . . . so, I actually do not thing you are right with that comment - at least not for this band.*

*I hope your trip was a good one.*

*Very best,*

*Heather*

Whoops. This is where my innate instinct to shit all over hard-working people who just want to play a European Soccer Championship halftime show typically backfires. So while it looked like I completely fucked up any chance of getting in with a rising superstar indie band, of course charming Trin and his Trin-tastic smile ended up tweeting OMAM's female lead, Nanna Bryndís Hilmarsdóttir, a few months later and got an immediate reply.

**Trin's tweet:** "Hey, my name's Trin. I'm so pretty"

**[OK, I don't have his original tweet, but I'm sure it was something like that. The rest is real.]**

**Nanna's tweet:** "Thank you Matthew! (that sort of rhymed) enjoy life in Europe! There are some beautiful places to be seen!"

**Trin's tweet:** "It's been incredible! Iceland may be my favorite . . . actually stayed in Raggi's old apt"

**Nanna's tweet:** "hahaha Yeah we notised that it was being rented out for travelers. Was the guestbook above the toilet still there?"

**Trin's tweet:** "haha don't think so. but paintings are still on the walls. Had to get help translating . . ."

S

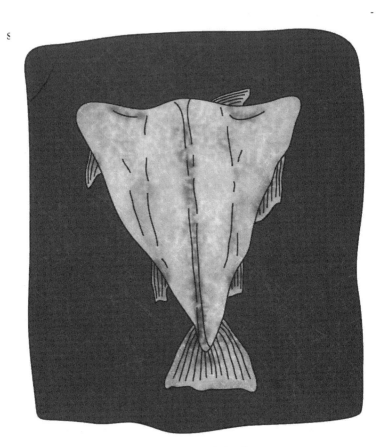

*"Lífið er Saltfiskur"*
*Illustration © SiggaRún, 2013*

# ELEVEN

# Protectors of the Earth

Remember Arna from the second chapter? The red-haired love of my life? After that night, I stayed in touch with her on Facebook because 1) the obvious, and 2) her mother's tours of the hidden people's favored locations. The hidden people's influence appeared all over the country, from elf figurines sold in grocery stores to hulking troll statues by the side of the highway. Americans who hear that half of the Icelandic refuse to deny the existence of elves never fail to raise an eyebrow (which is bizarre since nine out of 10 Americans believe a magic man in the sky created them and actively controls events in their lives). This fervent belief in the invisible civilizations hiding in the lava rocks continued to pique my curiosity throughout our trip. I convinced Trin and Bojo to go on an elves tour with Arna's mom.

Now remember Inga? From Akureyri? Luckily, she lived in the nearby the town of Hafnarfjörður and had come to hang out with us in Reykjavík to have a—ahem—sleepover with Trin. The next day she offered to drive us to Hafnarfjörður so we wouldn't have to mess with the bus.

"Inga," said Bojo. "MVP of the trip."

We killed some time in Hafnarfjörður at the Viking Festival, which just happened to have started that day. Little kids got lessons on how to sword fight with sticks in Viking fashion while craftsmen hawked their wares, from knives to earrings to whalebone necklaces. We struck up a conversation with a woman who acted as some kind of Viking fortune-teller. She gathered stones in a small purse and had us each pick one. I selected the Tree of Life, which seemed to be a good thing. Trin's denoted "mental and physical hardship," so she let him pick again.

"Oh, sure, just keep picking until you get Tree of Life," I complained. "Gonna take your ball and go home if you don't get Tree of Life."

It would have been nice to stay for a leg of pig, which was slow-roasting over some coals on a spit, but other than the spike running through its mouth and anus the creature looked almost alive, so we went to meet Arna's mom in front of the town hall.

When we arrived, she had a grocery bag for us.

"A girl told me to give this to you. It's a traditional Icelandic travel lunch," she said.

That morning while we ate breakfast Inga had explained the typical Icelandic travel lunch, which included roast lamb on thin pita-like bread with butter and a box of chocolate milk. We kidded her that this was probably bullshit, and she just wanted to see what she could get three American guys to eat.

"Inga," I said now that I held a traditional Icelandic travel lunch, "for real, MVP of the trip!"

Arna's mom was named Sibba Karlsdóttir,

**[A rather important note on Icelandic surnames that I probably should have brought up in the first chapter: The Icelandic do not have standard surnames passed down through the family patriarch. Rather the patriarch's first name carries on to the children with "son" or "daughter" as the suffix (i.e. "dottir" for daughter). So my dad would have been named "Bob Henryson" and I would have been "Stephen Bobson." Charlie Sheen would be "Charlie Martinson" and Drew Barrymore, "Drew Johnsdaughter" and so forth. This is a great explanation of why the Icelandic need Incest Facebook, but more on this later.]**

and she was a short, stout woman of around 50 with short gray hair and a streak of red running through the bangs. She had a soft, mellifluous voice that was pitch perfect for rattling off folklore. Her elf tours, which she had been doing for 11 years, had made her a minor celebrity around town. Hafnarfjörður, she explained, was the capital of the elves, many of which lived in the crags and outcroppings of a nearby cliff, and though she'd started the tours to earn a little extra money, they proved enduringly popular. She'd appeared on several international news shows, including BBC and NPR.

Three Germans and a British mom and her son gathered with us for the tour, and we began a slow stroll around town, with our first stop a large boulder in a residential neighborhood. Hafnarfjörður, she explained, was replete with huge rocks just left on the lawns. This one had a rusting spike protruding from its core. The man who'd built the nearby house in 1920 had hired several workers to break up the rock. All of them had failed: one driving a spike in and finding himself unable to dislodge it, and another breaking his leg. Eventually, the homebuilder came to understand that this rock served as a home for elves and left it alone. There it sits still.

"An American journalist came here a few years back," said Sibba. "She asked many people if they believed in the elves. Some said yes, some said no, of course, but the ones who said no, she asked them, 'Would you be willing to break up one of these rocks that are supposedly the elves' homes?' All of them said no. Just in case."

Sibba explained that there were many types of hidden people, from elves to dwarves to trolls, and even among the elves, there were subcategories, some of whom walked among humans, held jobs, and could be identified by missing nostril cartilage. Not everyone can see elves. It takes a seer, someone with "the third eye" to detect them. She went on to tell us all kinds of hidden people and elf stories; some of which live on as half-realized summaries in my notes, but I went to the internet to pull a few that offer an explanation of how seriously the Icelandic take their elves. When building a highway near Reykjavík in the 1970s, a number of delays and mishaps caused the government to hire a clairvoyant to negotiate with the elves. This is not unusual: Many municipalities like Hafnarfjörður have discussions on village planning councils about the interests of the hidden people. Even after that psychic cleared the construction of the highway, though, a bulldozer moving a rock that was supposedly an elf home fractured a water pipe that ended up killing thousands of trout hatchlings on a fish farm.

Sibba told us of a nearby golf course where the negotiations went better. After a number of setbacks and minor disasters plaguing the construction of the course, the primary engineer went out to the course to mollify the elves. After speaking to them, "showing them kindness," as Sibba put it, the project carried on without incident.

The hidden people can be mischievous, as when they snatch or borrow eyeglasses or a pair of scissors, only to return them later to a completely different location. Or they can be downright beneficent. Sibba told us the story of a boy who fell down a cliff of the mountain that towers over Hafnarfjörður. He spoke of how hands came out of the cliff face and carried him down the side, delivering him to the ground with little more than a few scratches. The doctor who treated him, Sibba said, did not believe in elves, "but he also said, he didn't have a better explanation for how the boy survived at all—let alone with so few injuries."

Like Jón Gnarr explained, to understand the Icelandic attachment to the folk tales of hidden people, you must understand a bit of Icelandic history—why the people of this island nation enjoy the idea that nature has its guardians. It's easiest to begin with the story of the American aluminum company Alcoa.

In the 1990s, as the Icelandic government worked to create investment potential, they decided on a plan to sell Iceland's enormous reserves of glacial rivers and geothermal power to foreign companies in energy-intensive industries like Alcoa. They dammed most of the country's major rivers and built a vast network of infrastructure—not just dams but tunnels deep underground that would carry water to hydropower stations, as well as electrical transmission lines to reach the smelter on the coast. Massive amounts of pristine wilderness were drowned in the process, and the smelters emitted pollution (though the electricity is still zero emissions) all for what amounted to a few hundred jobs in the remote east of the country. Now one can argue about the trade-offs: Those few hundred jobs do support economic activity in the sparsely populated east versus the destruction of habitat where reindeer calved.

What was interesting, however, is that while many Icelanders didn't like the project, they also didn't exactly rise up in protest either. The free market Independence Party continued to rule while the left-leaning Social Democratic Alliance continued to founder, unable to find a way to mount a serious challenge. However, before the Alcoa plant could begin construction, the company had to agree to allow a "government expert" to investigate the plant site and certify that no elves were living on the land, under the land, or near the land. Imagine if BP had an exorcist zooming around in a boat before it went drilling for oil in the Gulf.

Yet the story is not just weird—it's apocryphal. The Alcoa plant got built, but Iceland remains a nation in thrall to the results of its near-catastrophic environmental past. Wherever the origins of stories of the hidden people first arose—Gnarr's Irish monks being the most likely explanation—there are well-founded historical and scientific origins of the Icelandic caution in overburdening pieces of the natural world.

By roughly 700 c.e. the Scandinavian homeland had come under population stress. Arable land for new farming to support the expanding population had largely vanished, and coupled with improved boat technology, including the advent of sails, Scandinavian chieftains looked to expand westward. Viking settlers in Iceland, overwhelmed by the seeming abundance of the land they'd discovered, went about grazing and felling the trees with zeal. Remember that wood wasn't just the basis for building structures; it was also used to make charcoal, which the Vikings needed to craft iron. Four pounds of wood makes roughly one pound of charcoal. Almost unbelievably, however, much of the forest the Vikings cleared was just burned or wasted. In *Collapse*, Jared Diamond explains how approximately 80 percent of Iceland's original woodlands were cleared in the initial decades of colonization and 96 percent by the 20th century. Today, only 1 percent of the entire country remains forested. It's hard not to make a direct analogy to the way modern societies blow through petroleum and other fossil fuels as if these resources have no limit (not to mention, fisheries, forests, soil, and just about everything else).

What the Vikings didn't understand was that Iceland's soil was different from their Scandinavian home; it had accumulated slowly and was more fragile. The rich capital of soil and vegetation did not replenish itself as fast in this alien country, and in just a few centuries, the settlers had managed to deforest the entire island and plunge their society into a serious environmental crisis. Much of the country still retains that look of a barren moonscape—so much so that NASA used it to train astronauts for what they would encounter on the moon while sci-fi films like *Prometheus* make use of the cold, desert-like landscape. Until the introduction of modern building materials in the last century, the Icelandic built almost everything out of sod and driftwood. Coupled with a cool climate, shorter growing season, and the occasional volcanic eruption that scattered ash over the island and poisoned everything, Iceland had several extremely rough centuries. People starved, they fled, they died. Only through enormous collective effort did their ancestors pull together to find ways to survive. They did this by making fish a dietary staple. The settlers exterminated basically everything else—seabirds, walruses, and seals. The barnyard animals overgrazed the land, so the only source of protein was the plentiful stocks of cod and haddock. As previously noted, the introduction of motorized boats led to an explosion in industrial-scale fishing by the early 1900s and with it came Iceland's first taste of prosperity. Or as a Halldór Laxness character from another novel put it, "When all is said and done, life is first and foremost salt fish."

To this day, the Icelandic government remains in constant battle with the ghosts of its past. As Diamond points out, the government has an entire department dedicated to retaining soil, regrowing woodlands, revegetating the interior, and regulating sheep stocks. Even so, the soil continues to erode into the sea at an alarming rate while the government pays farmers to plant trees—a never-ending race to get the roots to take hold and secure the soil. Any spot of forest gets treated with near reverence, and Iceland actually has a so-called "Tree of the Year," awarded each year to— you guessed it—an impressive and sturdy tree. On the tour, Sibba took us to the 2007 recipient, a gnarly behemoth that had grown over a stone wall, its branches extending in a canopy of claws over the small road.

What's so patently obvious is that Iceland's struggles are a mere microcosm of the battle the entire planet will have to undertake as our glaciers sluice into the sea, our rainforests are felled, unimaginable metric tons of carbon spew into the atmosphere, millions of tons of toxins spill into our water, fisheries collapse, and top soil, as in Iceland, vanishes.

Economists call it a tragedy of the commons: People insist on their freedom to denude their "private property" in any way they wish, to horde the wealth they pull from the land or sea, and while the party's going strong, no one much cares what the repercussions may be.

Iceland's independent people thought they could all graze as many sheep and fell as many trees as they wished without consequence and in doing so nearly destroyed their entire society.

As another character in Laxness' *Independent People* points out, "The love of freedom and independence has always been a characteristic of the Icelandic people. Iceland was originally colonized by freeborn chieftains who would rather live and die in isolation than serve a foreign king."

One can't help but think it might be better if there really were a hidden people peeping out from crevices in the rocks, watching for egregious violations of the unseen pact between humanity and the natural world it exploits for wealth and warmth and happiness. It would be nice to have someone to watch us, the spoiled children that we sometimes resemble, to smack our hands when we reach for something that we ought not. Unfortunately, there is only us, absently hoping that the majority come around, as the Icelandic did, before it's all too late.

**The Pride of Iceland**
*Illustration © SiggaRún, 2013*

# TWELVE

# Reyk City

*"Who are they? A couple of brazen-faced young sluts, of course, fit for nothing but parading the streets and living on their parents like parasites."*

—Bjartur of *Summerhouses*

Bojo, who has a near-autistic knowledge of hip-hop, immediately dubbed Reykjavík, "Reyk City."

**Inside Joke #9,788:** "Reyk City" being a play on the Tyga song "Rack City," which includes the lyric "Rack City, bitch, Rack-Rack City, bitch." This obviously became us walking around rapping to each other, "Reyk City, bitch, Reyk-Reyk City, bitch."

Without a doubt, you had to be there.

Our last days in Reykjavík were spent in a stupor, a funtastic fog, drunken and exhausted. We tried to take in as much of the city as we could while still accomplishing life stuff. I was, nominally, still working from the road while Bojo and Trin had to plan the next leg of their trip to the U.K. and Ireland. Also, we had to go out. We had to go out a lot.

**Iceland Travel Tip #566:** There are a lot of bars in Reykjavík, and the Icelandic take them very seriously. As the video-store clerk with a limitless pool of knowledge told us, the young people in Reykjavík do not have bar loyalty. They go to whatever the new hip place is. For my money, it all depends on what you're looking for. If you want to see the hottest Icelandic women you can possibly find, there's a place called B5 (Bar Five), which will remind you a lot of your standard American douche-bag, ass-grinding repository. It's the kind of place where dudes with a lot of money hang out, and judging by the eternal line outside, it was the most popular place in the city.

On our first night Bryndís told us, "Oh, you want to see skinny girls who like Americans, go to the B5. They are all sticks, and they will like you if you just go up and tell them, 'Hey, baby, you come home with me now.'"

This, to say the least, is not my style. I grew up in dive bars, and for this, Reykjavík has plenty of options. The aforementioned Prikið became our go-to place, and I highly recommend its musical stylings, swinging lights, and labyrinthine style. Lewbowski was also a great deal of fun, but that might have had a lot to do with our bartender, who we flirted with the entire night, and who looked so startlingly like the actress Hayden Panettiere, you could almost believe in an indestructible cheerleader.

**Iceland Travel Tip #349:** Even with the krónur devalued, Iceland is still an expensive place to eat and drink. There's not really much you can do to get around the price of alcohol. Iceland basically had prohibition on alcohol from 1915 until 1935, and after that the only beer that was sold had an alcohol content of less than

2.25 percent, which is a lower than the crappy three-two beer my parents tell me about. How would you even get a buzz going on 2.25 percent beer? You'd have to drink a vat of it. Not until March 1, 1989 (1989!) could you even drink real beer in Iceland. Bars would sell a non-alcoholic pilsner with vodka mixed in it. Now they celebrate March 1 as Beer Day. However, alcohol and tobacco still fall under control of a state monopoly, which only sells them at 46 designated stores called "Vínbúðin." "Vínbúðin" was one of the only words I learned well. The Vínbúðin only stays open until 6 p.m., though, so if you forget to buy your alcohol during the day, you're screwed. Furthermore, the tax is based on alcohol content, so a bottle of whiskey becomes prohibitively expensive.

## Characters

We met a fantastic array of characters in our final five days, some of whom I will list now:

**Super-Beautiful Demure Geysir Cashier and Björk Backup Singer:** Super-Beautiful Demure Geysir Cashier and Björk Backup Singer was actually named Ásdís, and Trin interviewed her for his website GiveLiveExplore. Trin met Ásdís the first day he and Bojo were in Reykjavík while she worked at her job behind the cash register of the Icelandic clothing store Geysir. He chatted her up and found out that she sang in a choir that had backed up Björk on her last album. She'd spent the previous year traveling the world with Iceland's most famous pop star.

This led us to create the game "1-degree of Björk" since it seemed as if everyone in Iceland either casually knew the woman who lived on her own island off the coast or knew at least one person who did. For instance, Mayor Gnarr's wife was a good buddy of Björk.

Anyway, we grilled Ásdís on what it was like to sing for Björk (cool), what it was like to travel the world with a touring pop star (good), what her favorite place was (Brazil), and what Björk was like (nice). Overall, Ásdís should have bragged much more about her extremely cool 1-degree of Björk connection.

**Fake NBA Player and Posse:** The whole time we were out and about in Reykjavík we kept running into this group of black American guys, including one who was extremely tall—maybe 6 feet 8 inches. As we all know, everyone just assumes that if you're 6-foot-8 and black, you play basketball. In this case, however, after we'd finally run into these guys enough times, we asked what their deal was, and they said that the guy was, indeed, an NBA player for the Sacramento Kings, and the rest of them were his old friends and business manager. Colloquially known as a "posse."

Since I'm obsessed with the NBA, it was love at first sight for me, and I begged the guy to let me interview him for my blog, to which he agreed. His name was Matt; I didn't recognized him, but the NBA is full of guys filling out the end of the roster—journeymen who never see playing time and undrafted rookies fighting to break into the rotation, so I figured it was plausible. Bojo and Trin looked him up, however, and couldn't find him. After several more run-ins it finally came out that these guys were not an NBA basketball player and his posse, but just a bunch of guys who were tall and black and on vacation in Iceland.

"People just kept assuming that," said Matt. "It got easier to tell them that's who we were."

"Plus, I bet it didn't hurt with girls," I noted.

"We definitely smushed while we were here," he admitted. "But I doubt my occupation would have made a difference."

So I didn't blame them for the fib. Plus, they turned out to be cool dudes, and we partied at Prikið our last night in town. Also, one of the guys had lived in Chicago for a few years and lit up when he found out I was a columnist for RedEye. This meant that, technically, I turned out to be the famous guy they met in Iceland and not the other way around.

**Bam Margera:** While in Prikið on a Saturday night, I muscled my way to the bar to buy a drink. The guy I sidled up next to looked familiar, and it took me a few drunken seconds to realize it was Bam Margera of *Jackass* fame. He kind of nodded at me, and I nodded back and promptly forgot about it.

**Talking Politics with Some Icelandic Kid:** While hanging out in Lebowski, we met these guys. Meeting big groups of guys can sometimes be hugely advantageous. Lebowski had a "wheel" you could spin for a few hundred krónur, and most of the time you ended up winning huge volumes of shots or beer. The guys kept spinning and winning, so at one point I had two shots and three full beers sitting in front of me, which led to much rejoicing, huzzahing, and American-style high-fiving. Bojo, Trin, and I only paid for a single beer the whole night.

In the course of this time, I struck up a conversation with an Icelandic guy, who for lack of any other memorable descriptor, we'll call Some Iceland Kid. He was very interested in hearing about my interview with Gnarr, talking melting glaciers, and

American presidential elections. Finally, he brought up this weird story:

Apparently, a Chinese billionaire named Huang Nubo was attempting to buy up a huge portion of northeastern Iceland that would link the Vatnajökull and Jökulsárgljúfur national parks—right where we'd just traveled a few days earlier. Nubo was chairman of the Zhongkun investment group and former minister of the Chinese Central Propaganda Department.

**[China, don't you think you could at least make an effort to pretend that you don't have entire government departments devoted to misrepresenting reality to your citizens? Call it like the "Department of Happy Fun Cherry Ice Cream." Anything.]**

Nubo wanted to build a luxury hotel and eco-resort with a focus on "nature conservation and environmental tourism." He offered a billion krónur along with a promise to invest 20 billion more, but the Icelandic had concerns and first made Huang renounce water rights to the Jökulsá á Fjöllum river (which runs right into our favorite waterfall, Dettifoss). Despite a need for foreign investment following its banking crisis, Iceland was dubious about selling 300 square kilometers of land to a Chinese tycoon with links to the government, especially given China's global spending spree of buying up strategic positions and whatnot.

Huang said his motives were pure: He had an Icelandic roommate in college at Peking University, and pointed out that he donated a million dollars to set up an Icelandic-Chinese poetry exchange program.

[I'm torn here because the term "Icelandic-Chinese poetry exchange program" led me to come up with too many jokes, and I couldn't tell how many of them were racist or not.]

The Icelandic government rejected Huang's proposal in November 2011.

Nevertheless, by the time I had a conversation with this kid, he reported to me that Iceland may lease the land to Huang for 99 years and allow him to build his resort.

**My Unrequited Icelandic Love:** I was beginning to feel a bit lame that I hadn't made inroads with any Icelandic women since arriving. To be sure, I was not out to get laid as a specific goal, but I understood what Bryndís was talking about when it came to Americans in Iceland: I felt like an NBA basketball player. I've never been in a country where the women walk up to you and ask to buy you drinks.

[Also, they have this really cute thing they do where—while in a noisy, crowded bar—they put a thumb over your ear before talking into it. Both thoughtful and totally adorable.]

Still, as we'd traveled, way too many people had told us how much we would have to suck to not hook up with an Icelandic woman. For instance, our wise video store clerk said to us, "Oh, you would have to be a retarded to not get Iceland woman home with you. You must be aggressive. Don't give them a choice."

Now as I explained, that's not really my thing, and I find it incredibly disconcerting that a video store clerk was advising us to do everything short of raping a woman to get her attention.

Nevertheless, on Saturday night in Prikið, after I'd had my interaction with Bam Margera, I went upstairs to the bathroom. I was extremely drunk, and the advice of Bryndís and the video store clerk throbbed in my head. Upon walking out, I spotted a very, very attractive young woman with short brunette hair, dark eyebrows, and small tombstone teeth. Our eyes met, and before I really understood what I would say, I'd walked up to her and kind of yelled into her face, "Hey! You're so beautiful I want to eat your panties!"

She smiled. "Uh, what are these? What are 'panties'?" she asked.

I pointed to her hip. "Your underwear!" I explained. "I want to eat your underwear!"

At this, she threw her head back and laughed.

"You are funny," she said. "Can I buy you drinks?"

"Yes," I said, as she took my hand and led me through the crowd. "Yes, you can."

It's like how when a local Icelandic leader named Thorbjorg beseeched Grettir the Strong as to why he had come to his town to stir up such trouble. Grettir replied, "I had to be somewhere."

**Errant Icelanders We Mistakenly Took Back to Our Apartment:** On Sunday, two days before we left, we found ourselves back in Vegamót where we met a big group of Icelanders who were the only people hanging out in the place. We sat and drank with them for a few hours. Two of them were extremely pretty blond girls, and one was an extremely pretty Asian girl, so naturally we ended up inviting them back to our apartment for an after-party, and naturally, the pretty girls all seemed to melt away to be replaced by a bunch of weirdos. This happens at a lot of after-parties. You have to understand, though, this one girl was in the Steve Markley Wheelhouse: just blond and sexy as sin.

"I like your pants," I said as my moronic opening line, and from there we were talking. After a while, she brought up that we weren't the only Americans in Iceland. She'd heard Tom Cruise and Bam Margera were in town.

"Oh, yeah. I saw Bam Margera at Prikið last night. We nodded at each other."

"Oh my God," she cried. "Are you serious?"

"Uh . . . yeah?"

"Oh my God. Oh my God," she said, fluttering her hands at her face, looking genuinely hot and bothered. "Oh my God, he is my boyfriend. Bam is like the sexiest man ever. Oh my God, you saw him?"

"Yep," I said. "Wait, really? The *Jackass* guy is the sexiest man ever?"

"Are you kidding? Bam, he is my boyfriend. I want him so bad."

And she went on to talk about Bam Margera until she got too wasted at our apartment and her friends had to take her home, which just goes to show . . . well, something about fame and human sexuality, but I'll be damned if I can figure out what.

Unfortunately in our haste to get two to three pretty girls back to our apartment, we ended up with a whole slew of other people who wouldn't leave.

This included a loud, abrasive young woman who did not stop talking until she passed out on the couch where I was supposed to sleep. She also went down to the garden to smoke a cigarette where she got into a loud argument with another apartment-dweller at 4 a.m., and Trin had to go run interference, at which point he almost got into it with this guy over this loud, stupid girl who was definitely in the wrong and who we really wanted to leave.

This included a pleasant, mild-mannered, portly University of Iceland philosophy major, who was amazed that he'd met an American writer and who was great fun to talk to about the nature of reality until it was 5 a.m. Then we'd drank everything in the house, smoked weed, all basically passed out, and he was still at our place, unwilling to understand that it was time to close down the whole operation.

This included a very strange brother-sister combo. The Sister was one of the aforementioned beautiful young women we didn't mind having back to our apartment because she had outrageously great breasts. The Brother was a red-haired moron/fool/douche bag, who Bojo suspected disappeared into our bathroom to do coke. The Sister worked at Vegamót and the Brother was a "DJ," which I'm sure means he lived with his parents. He kept wiping at his nose and expressing his undying love for club music, repeating himself enough times that I felt stupid pretending like he hadn't just said what he'd already said moments earlier. Brother and Sister had kind of a weird interaction-relationship going on. I realize we were all drunk, but they were just too touchy-feely-teasy to not make the three of us uneasy. It also didn't help that while we were sitting around our living room, the Brother flat out asked us, "Which one of you wants to fuck my sister?"

At which point she slapped him and said, "Oh! You are so silly!"

And to which, I was thinking, *Only if you take a lie-detector test swearing that you will not think about it later while jerking off.*

It actually turned out that not only was the Brother undoubtedly in our bathroom doing coke, but that he took that time to vomit into a towel and hide it at the bottom of the laundry basket. Later, the lady we rented from would inform us of this unpleasant discovery.

Which leads me to:

**Iceland Travel Tip #21:** Although this was only one experience, I would caution Americans traveling in Iceland that perhaps the Icelandic, once invited to a party, have a hard time taking what we call "a hint." Again, not to indict an entire nationality, but by 6 in the morning we all had to just go to bed and hope that these people wouldn't rob us or, like, have incest on the carpet.

[A fascinating addendum to this story that I didn't find out until much, much later: The woman who owned the apartment had a little girl, and Trin actually retired to the little girl's bedroom with the Sister where they began making out. However, things then went very wrong. It was a combination of this girl's body being quite phenomenal, her saying such specifically dirty, sexually aggressive things to him, and Trin having smoked pot for the first time in six years. Despite our assurances that there were no prostitutes in Iceland, Trin became hyper-paranoid and convinced himself mid-make-out that the Sister was actually a prostitute and Brother was her pimp, and that if they actually hooked up the Brother would come looking for his money. So instead of hooking up with this incredibly good-looking

**girl, Trin got super-terrified-paranoid and pretended to go to sleep. I will forever feel an enormous amount of *Schadenfreude* about that.]**

## National Day

We had arranged to be in Reykjavík for National Day, which is the equivalent of their Fourth of July. I woke up that morning to find a note from Bojo and Trin sitting outside my door, along with an onion (It's important to note that we'd agreed if any of us failed to fool around with a lady on our trip, we would have to wear some Justin Bieber tattoos we found in the apartment):

> *Dear Steve,*
>
> *Congrats on averting the Biebs tattoo. We're going to that Kaffi shop (same one as yesterday) until about 2 p.m. Then heading to City Hall @ 2 for some National Day shit. Prob be at City Hall from 2-3:30ish. Then we'll come back here. I'll email if our plans change.*
>
> *Love,*
> *Mike + Matt*
>
> *P.S. Here's an onion.*

I wandered out into Reyk City to find them. The streets were packed, and the country's flag, a red and white cross in a rectangle of blue flew from windows, cars, and poles. Like America, many dressed in patriotic colors. Multiple stages across the city center hosted bands, and the streets were lined with rides, games, and blow-up playgrounds for children. There were gymnasts, street performers, and Icelandic strong-men competitors.

[For a country of 320,000, Iceland actually wins a disproportionate number of World's Strongest Man competitions and beauty pageants. The former being where behemoth dudes drag big rig trucks and throw dumbbells 12 feet in the air or whatever. Obviously, you can see the Viking influence there, but Iceland's other secret—and why its women tend to be so pretty—has to do with the origins of the Icelandic colony. It began as a Viking outpost, but before heading to Iceland, the Vikings stopped off in Ireland and "married" (read, "kidnapped") all the most beautiful Irish women. Ninth-century Ireland's terror is Iceland's gain today in Miss Universe trophies.]

I feel obliged to tell the story of National Day, but to explain why National Day lands on June 17, 1944, even though the Icelandic people can all trace their roots back to the first settlers in the ninth and 10th centuries, I'll have to get in to a whole thing here. And as we all know, no one likes to learn about history unless it stars really famous American film actors. Therefore, this subsection will be titled:

## Wikipedia's Icelandic History as Portrayed by Famous American Film Actors

As Jón Gnarr mentioned in our interview, it is now widely believed that Irish monks arrived in Iceland before the Nordic settlers, but because they were just a bunch of dudes who couldn't have babies, they either died or got wiped out by the Vikings. Archeological evidence and radiocarbon dating confirmed a settlement near Keflavík that was probably abandoned between 770 and 880 c.e. before Norse settlement began in 874. Although a slew of these badasses made it over to "Snowland," it was Arnold Schwarzenegger (Flóki Vilgerðarson) who became the first Scandinavian to deliberately spend some time on the northeastern coast during the winter. At this point the Norse Terminator must have been freezing his balls off so thoroughly that when he saw ice drifting around in the fjords, he bitterly, frigidly gave the landmass the name *Ísland* or Iceland.

Following Schwarzenegger, a Norwegian chieftain named Sylvester Stallone (Ingólfr Arnarson) led his mighty clan to settle the island permanently. Legend has it that he threw two pillars of wood overboard and swore he'd settle wherever they washed up. They washed up on a peninsula that Stallone named the Cove of Smoke because of the geothermal activity, and to this day the city of *Reykjavík* stands because Cobra wanted to chase two pieces of wood to shore. Much of this history comes to us from the Book of Settlement (Landnámabók), which was written 300 years after Stallone arrived, at which point he might have Tangoed his way into history as the first settler when really it was Kurt Russell (Náttfari), who simply failed to Cash in.

In 60 years, settlers fleeing an over-crowded Norway ruled by the tyrannical king Harald the Fair-Haired (Thomas Jane?) had settled most of the arable land, and they brought with them Scottish and Irish slaves.

By 930, the ruling chieftains established what is considered one of the oldest democratic systems in the world after the Roman Empire. It was called the Althing.

[*Thing* means "assembly" and the current Icelandic parliament is still called the Althing and traces its roots back to the first chieftains. Ironically, I spent much of our time in Reykjavík wondering where the Althing was until I finally looked it up and learned that we'd been

**driving and walking by it our whole stay. It simply looks less like a parliamentary building than it does a museum for handcrafted candles or antique doll furniture.]**

The Althing met in Thingerville, the lush plain where the continental plates meet, a valley run through with estuaries, small islands, and sizable walls of stone that create little hallways of rock. This, you'll recall, is where the duck attacked us. Before vicious ducks scared them off, the chieftains met each summer to settle quarrels, brush up laws, and create juries to settle lawsuits. Instead of writing laws down, a Lawspeaker would recite a third of the laws each summer, so that every three years you got to hear this guy tell you everything that could get you in trouble. There was no army or police force to compel anyone to obey the laws, however, and no executive office tasked with carrying out the rule of law, so mostly rival chieftain clans just murdered each other over their interpretations. This is gruesomely depicted in the Icelandic Sagas, which will someday surely get an option from HBO. When we visited Thingerville, I read some of the violent descriptions of executions that took place there. Drowning, for instance, was a preferred method of execution. For some reason, women specifically were often executed this way: tied up in a sack and held under the water of a pool or river until they were dead. Which I guess is no more violent or disturbing than anything that was happening on mainland Europe at the time.

Now the chieftains weren't exactly rulers. Farmers could ally themselves with one chieftain or another, but they could switch allegiances at will and this gave the powerful some incentive to treat their people well in order to widen their spheres of influence.

In this way, the system differed greatly from mainland Europe's feudal setup.

The people of Iceland had a pagan heritage and mostly worshipped guys like Chris Hemsworth (Thor) and Anthony Hopkins (Odin), but Christianity had stampeded through Europe and there was great pressure for the Icelandic to convert and worship Jim Caviezel (Jesus Christ). By the 10th century, tensions were running high, so the Althing appointed Mel Gibson (Þorgeirr Ljósvetningagoði) to hash out the issue of whether the people should worship Hemsworth and Hopkins and the rest or switch to Caviezel. Gibson picked Caviezel.

During the next 200 years, families and clans grew larger and more powerful, denuding the parliamentary nature of the Althing. Beginning in 1200, one specific family began to consolidate power: the Sheens (the Sturlungs). This is known as "the Age of the Sheens" (the Age of the Sturlungs). Martin (Sturla Þórðarson) and his sons Charlie (Sighvatur) and Emilio Estevez (Snorri) sowed chaos and death across the land, bringing more and more farmers under their power. Then in 1220, Emilio Estevez made a deal with the king of Norway to become his vassal, and his nephew Charlie Sheen Jr. made a similar deal 15 years later. This led eventually to the Old Covenant, which brought Iceland under the vassalage of Norway. Still, the Althing persisted to make laws and hold trials while the Icelandic bishops grew more powerful. This all took place during the Little Ice Age when a climate shift turned the winters around the Arctic Circle harsher and growing seasons shorter, which (you'll recall) forced the population to turn to cod as a source of food and trade, which it remains to this day.

Things got shittier still, when in 1380 the Norwegian king died without having a son (For Caviezel's sake, you're the king! Just knock up one peasant!) and Norway became part of the Kalmar Union, which included Sweden but was really run by Denmark, those thugs. Denmark, you see, could give two shits about Iceland's cod fish, and as a result Iceland lost out on what little trade it had going. Perhaps not coincidentally, it was also during this period that the Greenland colony, nearly 500 years old, collapsed. The Protestant Reformation was also sweeping Europe, and the king of Denmark was forcing all his subjects to convert to Lutheranism. One of the Icelandic Catholic bishops, Mickey Rourke (Jón Arason), tried to fight back, but in 1550 Rourke was captured by forces loyal to the crown and got his head cut off. The rest of the country was like, "Lutheranism, it is!"

Being under Denmark's control blew for many other reasons. It imposed the Danish trade monopoly, which meant no one in Iceland could trade with any other nearby countries. Denmark sent few resources to protect the island, which in 1627 resulted in the Turkish Abductions when a fleet of pirates from the Ottoman Empire raided Iceland and kidnapped and enslaved 300 people. In 1660 Freddie Prinze Jr. (Frederick III) became the absolute monarch of Denmark-Norway and shut down any remnants of Icelandic autonomy.

Then in 1783, while Americans were celebrating becoming Americans, the Laki volcano erupted, spewing forth enough ash, lava, and fumes to kill 9,000 people on the spot. Worse, with 80 percent of the livestock wiped out, a famine swept the country, killing 25 percent of the small population. They call this the Mist

Hardships. Following the Napoleonic Wars, in order to settle all the shit Danny DeVito (Napoleon) had stirred up, Denmark and Norway were split into separate countries, but Denmark got to keep Iceland. The Icelandic were like, "Yeah, thanks for all that fucking help during the Mist Hardships, dickbags."

At this point, the Icelandic were pretty fed the fuck up with Denmark, and the first true independence movement emerged, led by a Danish-educated intellectual named A Young Paul Newman (Jón Sigurðsson). A Young Paul Newman helped re-establish the Althing as a consultative assembly in 1843. From there, total independence came piecemeal. By 1874, Denmark allowed Iceland self-rule and a constitution. By 1904, the constitution was expanded and a minister of Icelandic affairs in place. The 1918 Act of Union with Denmark recognized the Kingdom of Iceland as a sovereign state with Denmark representing the "kingdom" in foreign affairs and war.

Then came the Great War, also known as World War I, and much like *Bad Boys*, no one seemed to be asking for a sequel. The brutality and mass slaughter of the war greatly benefited Iceland, which profited from vastly increased demand for fish and whale oil.

[**Or as Bjartur of Summerhouses put it, "I only hope they go on blasting one another's brains out as long as other folk can get some good out of it. There ought to be plenty of people abroad. And no one misses them." Typical Bjartur.**]

The military protection of Denmark became a thing in 1940 when a group of people called the Nazis—you might have heard of them—occupied Denmark, and Iceland had to act fast, taking over its own foreign affairs and electing George Clooney (Sveinn Björnsson) provisional governor. They decided to kind of sort of invite/not get in the way of British forces landing in Reykjavík harbor. They simultaneously issued a protest at this violation of their neutral status while Prime Minister Bob Newhart (Hermann Jónasson) fumbled and muttered an announcement over the radio asking everyone to treat the invading troops politely.

World War II actually turned out to be the best thing to happen to Iceland in its history. When American troops replaced the British, they outnumbered all the Icelandic men in total and their presence basically eliminated unemployment. Following the war, Iceland got the most Marshall Plan money per capita of any country in Europe. Meanwhile, the Act of Union expired in 1943, and Iceland held a referendum in which 97 percent of voters agreed they should just go ahead and have their own country. Clooney was elected the first president on the day Iceland declared its independence, June 17, 1944. Danish King Zach Galifianakis (Christian X) sent a letter of congratulations.

***

Trin and I stopped to watch from the edge of a crowd as two street performers, one male and one female, balanced each other in preposterous fashions and then recruited men from the crowd to create a human table in which they all laid on each other while bent backwards at the knees. We strolled by City Hall and then turned up the main drag on our way to meet Bojo at a coffee shop.

"I feel like I could write a whole book about this place," I said.

"You should."

"Not like a real book. Not something I'd spend two years on and bleed my eyeballs out over, but something fun and fast, informative but mostly full of dick jokes and F-words. Publish it as an e-book and not even fuck around with a publisher."

"Yeah, man, that sounds great. Why not?"

"I don't know, why not?"

"Exactly."

I grinned.

"You're such a stupid optimist."

"I just get excited," Trin explained. "I think people should do things that excite them."

"This is going to be a much more abbreviated conversation if I actually write it down in the book, but will you help me?" I asked over the course of walking around for an hour on Iceland's most festive summer day.

"Sure, man," he said over the course of that hour. He also took me to task a bit. "You're such a funny, talented writer, but so totally hopeless when it comes to marketing yourself or getting the word out about your writing. That's the kind of stuff that excites me: entrepreneurship and building platforms and all that good stuff. You need to think about other methods, other avenues. And I think travel writing—not Rick Steves or anything like that—just Steve Markley going places and kind of making weird, Steve Markley observations—I'd read the shit out of that. Then who knows? Maybe if it sells enough, you go do one of these every year. Go to interesting places, learn about them, have Steve Markley-like adventures, write short e-books."

"Better than a real job," I agreed.

Our last night, Inga and Eygló came over to the apartment and cooked us a traditional Icelandic dinner complete with roasted lamb, vegetables, and potatoes. We sat around the tiny kitchen table, ate, and talked about the different places we were from, explaining Ohio and Hafnarfjörður in equal measure. I had the two of them show me their profiles on Incest Facebook, which is actually called Íslendingabók (or "Book of Icelanders"). Basically, you type in any two names, and it shows you how closely the two people are related in case they want to bang. Inga and Eygló showed me how they were eighth cousins.

I found Incest Facebook somewhat creepy, what with the complete unloading of people's private lives and genetic information into a publically available forum. Even if it does help you avoid having a genetically soupy kid, it hardly seems worth the trade-off.

"When it first started, it caused many problems," Inga told me. "People would see that they had brothers they had never heard of, and it was because their fathers had other families."

After dinner we put on Justin Bieber tattoos. The woman who'd rented us the apartment had a daughter, whose bed Trin had nearly hooked up on and who'd left some Bieber tattoos lying around—just little pictures of the Biebs with his face in a pink heart. I decided that no matter how much it might crush this little girl to lose her fake Bieber tattoos, we really needed to put them on before our last night out in Reyk City. We got one on Trin's chest, another on Bojo's arm, and Inga put one on the back of her hand. Because I'm much more daring than any of those losers, I opted for the tramp stamp, so now there are pictures of me hunched over in the kitchen, shirtless, while Bojo applies a Bieber tattoo to my lower back.

[Of course, I then promptly forgot about it, so that when I got back to New York, it still had not washed off. I was changing in front of my friend Anna days later when she cried out, horrified, "Did you get a tramp stamp? *And is it of Justin Bieber?*" What's even weirder is that when I landed at JFK I had to go down to the Financial District to get the keys to Anna's apartment where I was staying, but I got blocked from reaching her office because Justin Bieber himself was making an appearance in City Hall Park, and you could hear the screams of tween girls from Ground Zero five blocks away. So there I was walking right through the middle of a throng of prepubescent girls and the NYPD officers attempting to restrain them, onlookers of all ages watching in amusement, and I had this fake tattoo of Justin Bieber's face surrounded by a pink heart on my lower back. Life is so weird.]

My flight left early the next morning from Keflavík, and I'd calculated that I'd need to catch the 8 a.m. bus to make it. Nevertheless, we had to have a last hurrah. Prikið has a Monday night drinking club, so it was packed with Icelandic and tourists alike. The fake NBA player and his posse were there. Inga was there. A fight broke out and the participants were dragged into the streets. They played old American rap music from the '90s and early '00s, the era we all fell in love with it. The DJ's book of CDs looked almost identical to the one I owned in high school, and when I requested 2Pac's "California Love" everyone in the bar knew every word. The only song that got the natives more riled up was Sisqo's "Thong Song," which, I'm not exaggerating, sent them into orgiastic conniptions when it first blared through the speakers.

It was Trin's birthday, and we congratulated ourselves on keeping to our budget so well by buying many rounds. The fake NBA player bought me a shot. There was no dwelling.

And then we spilled out of the bar into the 1 a.m. daylight and staggered toward home. The cool night, jacket weather, cats, which seem to own Reykjavík, darting through the alleys, graffiti tagging stucco, adrift in all the white. I figure I'll get up around 6:30 a.m. just to give myself time to make it to the bus, but back in the apartment, we stay up rehashing the last of our inside jokes, maybe making some new ones that we promptly forget the next day, and we are still up at 3 in the morning, and I'm wondering if I should just plow through to the next day. When I do fall asleep, it's that blink-and-you're-awake kind of sleep. One moment Bojo's saying, "Goodnight, Steve. I love your Bieber tattoo," and the next he's beside you, shaking you awake because it's 7:30 and you were supposed to be up an hour earlier. And you're not even still drunk so much as stoned on your lack of sleep, and not just your lack of sleep that night but your lack of sleep for all these weeks when you never saw the sun fully set and the idea of night seemed a foreign concept. The light outside now looks exactly the same as when you crawled into bed. So you're racing through a shower, throwing your luggage together, dressing, innately understanding that if you miss this bus to Keflavík, you will miss your flight, and somehow this is bad—missed flights are bad—but it's all abstract bad, not specific bad, which somehow makes it worse because you can't even imagine the steps you'd have to take to rectify the situation. It's a psychic cliff and you can't picture what would be over the edge, though it would likely involve semi-drunken, sleepless negotiations with an Icelandair representative behind a ticket counter.

"Good luck, man," says your friend Bojo as you crash through the door with your suitcase. Stupid, responsible Bojo who somehow woke up for your flight when you didn't. And you don't even bother with Trin, likely spooning Inga, because you're probably going to miss this bus. Your friends will be on to other places: London, Scotland, Dublin, where they will make out with half-pretty Irish girls, the Icelandic having long ago robbed the best of the gene pool, and then Bojo will be onto the steel and rivers of Pittsburgh and Trin onto the wild yonder of Eastern Europe. And then you're out in the dawn, running along some unpronounceable one-way street with your backpack thudding against your back and the wheels of your rolly-suitcase thunking over the imperfections in the pavement, and everything is foggy and the air swims and the sun hides somewhere behind a cloud to the frozen north. And it's only now this place strikes you as the embodiment of those ever-warring human impulses, the ongoing spar between independence and community, freedom and collaboration, the Viking yearning clashing with the undeniable democratic power of the Althing, the bipolar nature of humankind somehow captured by these seasons of ultimate dark and ultimate light in the Cove of Smoke. It's now that you finally see them: at first nothing more than pairs of twin yellow in the dusky light. But they blink and emerge, from the ridges in the soft curves of grassy hills and from the rocks—they unfold from the rocks or come crawling slowly over the jagged surfaces, from crevices and hidey-holes indiscernible to the eye. They scamper toward you, knobs of knees and naked feet, scuttling over the grass and pavement to converge beside you, watching. And they urge you on, and that's when you drop the handle to the suitcase, just let it crash to a Reykjavík pavement and lie there beige and heavy and forgotten. And still they come, long spindly legs with knees and elbows like small flower bulbs, blinking at you, faces maybe curious but mostly blank, and you slough off the backpack, which hits the pavement with a crunch of books and iPad, but now you can actually pick up speed, and they all begin keeping pace beside you, wispy facial hair as fine as the down of a baby bird flowing back in the breeze, and you shed your jacket, feeling the chill of the country slip under your shirt, which you quickly tear off as well. You run faster to encourage the warmth, and they follow, watching. You pause only to kick off your shoes, and in one galvanic motion shove your jeans and underwear down, allowing it to carry off your socks, and the cold morning hits you in full force, like a breath mint enveloping your body, and now—finally—you can really sprint. You hurtle down the center of the road, not even sure of a destination anymore, street signs all inscrutable in this strange foreign tongue, and the wind whips at you, crawls on you, the cold tip of your penis seeming to point the way, your feet slapping at a surface that soon turns from pavement to dirt, from dirt to ancient lava. You sprint faster and faster until everything blurs in a volcanic mist. And still they run beside you, eternal, patient, watching.

# [Sources and Further Reading]

Clynes, Tom. "The Outlaw's Guide to Iceland." *National Geographic Adventure*. August, 2002.

Diamond, Jared. *Collapse: How Societies Choose to Fail or Succeed*. New York: Viking, 2005.

Halpern, Jake. "Iceland's Big Thaw." *The New York Times Magazine*. May 13, 2011.

Heath, Chris. "Iceland: Go with the Flow." *The Telegraph*. February, 2010.

Knight, Sam. "Caught Out." *Prospect*. July, 2011.

Lapidos, Julia. "Elf Detection 101: How to Find the Hidden People of Iceland." *Slate*. March 10, 2009.

Laxness, Halldór. *Independent People*. New York: Vintage International, 1946.

Lewis, Michael. *Boomerang: Travels in the New Third World*. New York: W.W. Norton & Company, 2011.

Lyall, Sarah. "Building in Iceland? Better Clear It With the Elves First." *The New York Times*. July 13, 2005.

Mala, Elisa. "Global Psyche: Magic Kingdom." *Psychology Today*. May 1, 2008.

McVeigh, Tracy. "The Party's Over for Iceland, the Island that Tried to Buy the World." *The Observer*. October 4, 2008.

Solnit, Rebecca. "News From Nowhere." *Harper's*. October, 2008.

Sunley, Christina. "Iceland's Stoic, Sardonic 'Independent People.'" *National Public Radio*. May 4, 2009.

Webster, Donovan. "Cod World." *Virginia Quarterly Review*. September, 2011.

# [GiveLiveExplore: Join Our Movement]

As we embarked on our trip to Iceland, we had no intention of documenting and sharing the tales of our journey. Yet this magical place nestled itself so deep into our hearts that we felt an obligation to tell the world about it.

Our purpose in sharing our *Tales* has become grander than just creating a fun book about Iceland—we'd prefer to create a movement. Our call to action is quite simple: **Visit Iceland.**

To further this call, we've created an online community of fellow Iceland-lovers at TalesofIceland.com. It's a visually stimulating site where anyone can share his or her own experiences in this remarkable country. If you've already visited Iceland, we'd love for you to share the "Tales" from your own journey. If you're planning a trip or simply dreaming about visiting Iceland, you'll find plenty of inspiration to kick your wanderlust into overdrive.

We've also compiled bonus material, like pictures from our road trip, Stephen's video interview with Jón Gnarr, and links to our favorite bars and restaurants in Iceland. These goodies and more can be found at: TalesofIceland.com/thebook.

# [About the Author]

With the debut of his first book at age 26, **Stephen Markley** garnered an immediate and devout cult following that has been growing since its publication. *Publish This Book: The Unbelievable True Story of How I Wrote, Sold, and Published This Very Book* (2010) has been an instant hit for writers, millennials, and anyone who enjoys a brazen sense of humor and a bold imagination. In 2011, he wrote and sold the screenplay and film rights to Kanea Arts Studio.

Markley went from an unknown author to having the third-best-selling nonfiction book in Chicago overnight, appearing in publications as varied as Psychology Today, the Writer Magazine, Booklist, the Huffington Post, USA Today, and the Boston Globe. During his book tour across the United States, Markley gathered rave reviews from media and other writers.

Markley has cultivated this following with his blog for the *Chicago Tribune*, "Off the Markley," which gets approximately 20,000 page views a month and includes subject matter covering everything from the perils of market liberalism to who would win in a fight between a puppy and a baby. His work for *RedEye* has made him one of its most popular columnists in the most widely circulated newspaper in Chicago.

In addition to the *Tribune* and *RedEye*, Markley's work has appeared in *The Week, Weber: A Study of the Contemporary*

*West*, *RadarOnline*, *Private Investigator's Magazine*, and Cars.com's blog KickingTires. His fiction has appeared in the *Chicago Reader*, *10,000 Tons of Black Ink*, and *Midnight Times*. He has appeared on WGN-TV and "The Alex and Amy Show" (formerly ChicagoNow Radio), and Radio DePaul. Exploiting Facebook, Twitter, YouTube, and every other social media advantage, Markley has developed a community of ardent fans, collecting thousands of emails and Facebook messages in just nine months of publication.

For more information, visit StephenMarkley.com.

# [Also By Stephen Markley]

## PUBLISH THIS BOOK: The Unbelievable True Story of How I Wrote, Sold, and Published This Very Book

Dear Reader-

This is called the "back cover copy," and you are no doubt familiar with its purpose. It describes what the book is about, so you can decide if you want to read it.

Here's the problem, though: I can't even describe this book, and I wrote the damn thing.

Basically, it's like this: fed up with the Byzantine quest of trying to publish a novel, I decide instead to cut to the chase and write a memoir about trying to publish a book-this book, to be precise.

Of course, now you're saying to yourself, "That is stupid," which is fair. But then you'll read it, and you'll say, "Damn, that was actually pretty good."

Because obviously it's about much more than just publishing a book. It's about life and love and friendship; politics, pop culture, and basketball; sex, drugs, and mild, inoffensive, slow-tempo Christian rock.

It's about the pitfalls of narrating your life as it unfolds, freaking out when an agent actually (spoiler alert!) takes an interest in this bizarre experiment, and the surreal shock you undergo when a publisher actually buys it and you suddenly realize that every secret drunk, drug, and sex story you've related will now be required reading for your parents, aunts, ex-girlfriends, and thousands of strangers who—you were kind of hoping—would never find out that you once accidentally shut your penis in a dresser drawer.

And finally, but most importantly, it's about those tumultuous early years of adulthood—the years when hope and fear and rage broil together and the promise of youth still holds the capacity to inspire awe. This is a story of those struggles—to find your true voice in your work and in your life. And the best part?

You pretty much know it has a happy ending.

## THE GREAT DYSMORPHIA: An Epistemological View of Ingesting Hallucinogenic Mushrooms at a 2012 Republican Debate

Norman Mailer. Hunter S. Thompson. David Foster Wallace.

All Stephen Markley ever wanted was a reason to use their names in a book blurb.

In November 2011, the nascent author and journalist attended a Republican presidential primary debate in Rochester, Michigan, wishing to see first-hand one of the most outlandish, jaw-dropping, eye-brow-raising primaries in American political history. The author of "Publish This Book" took his seat in the media filing center, set up his laptop, and uncapped the complimentary tin of M&Ms. Then he ate a bunch of hallucinogenic mushrooms.

After that, things—obviously—got weird.

From a verbal sparring match with the chaste being that resides behind Rick Santorum's sail-shaped nose to an encounter with bodyguards the size of Lone Star State cattle to a sweat-streaked, hair-tearing freak-out in a gymnasium shower stall, his experience inside the carnival theater of Election 2012's most memorable presidential debate will make you laugh, cry, dream, and despair. What Markley brought back from that debate is an essay not only about a political party and a presidential election but an entire rotten generation of policy perfidy and economic magical thinking —a report from an ideological faction with a demonstrated disconnect from reality that even Gore Vidal could not begin to appreciate. You know, unless he was on shrooms.

A perfect storm of youth and passion, recklessness and imagination, "The Great Dysmorphia" will take its place in the annals of unconventional, unbridled, uncensored, totally f***ing bizarre American campaign literature.

# [About GiveLiveExplore]

GiveLiveExplore is an independent publisher and lifestyle company that's obsessed with conscious travel and mindful exploration. Our anti-guidebooks are intended for the traveler who enjoys a fast, fun, educational read about foreign lands to compliment one's own travel experiences. Our intent is to provide useful cultural context through engaging storytelling, but still encourage all readers to explore the world and live out his or her own tales.

This was our goal with Stephen Markley's *Tales of Iceland*. Whether you're currently on a flight to Iceland, preparing for a holiday there, or simply dreaming of visiting one day, we hope you found this book entertaining and educational. It's the type of book we wish existed before our own trip to Iceland.

If you'd like to learn more about GiveLiveExplore and stay in touch with our upcoming projects, please visit GiveLiveExplore. com, or email Matt@GiveLiveExplore.com.

Thanks for joining us on this journey.

Matthew "Trin" Trinetti
Founder, GiveLiveExplore, LLC

25869405R00121

Made in the USA
Middletown, DE
12 November 2015